THE NEXT BIG THING

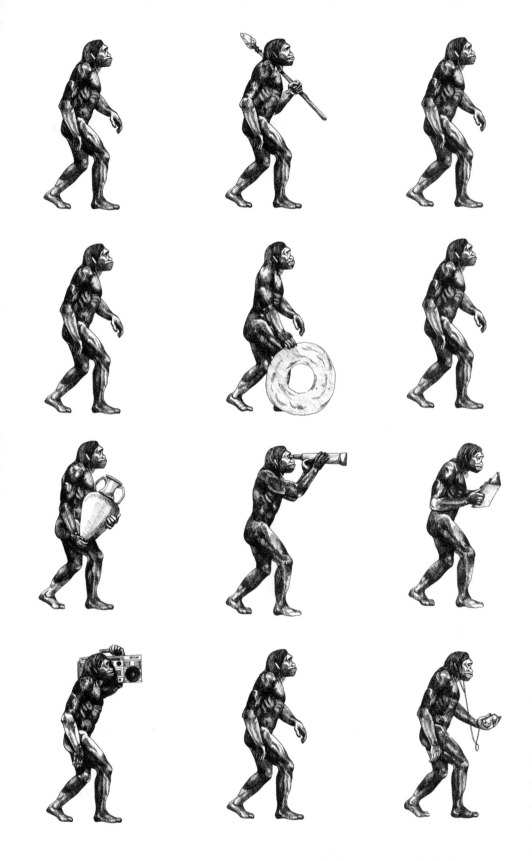

THE NEXT BIG THING

A HISTORY OF THE BOOM-OR-BUST
MOMENTS THAT SHAPED THE MODERN WORLD

— RICHARD FAULK —

ILLUSTRATIONS BY RAMSEY BEYER

ZEST BOOKS
San Francisco

Connect with Zest!

- zestbooks.net/blog
- zestbooks.net/contests
- twitter.com/zestbooks
- facebook.com/BooksWithATwist

35 Stillman Street, Suite 121, San Francisco, CA 94107 / www.zestbooks.net

Manufactured in the U.S.A.
DOC 10 9 8 7 6 5 4 3 2 1
4500512749

CONTENTS

INTRODUCTION

The next big thing. It's a marketing cliché as old as advertising itself — the wonder product that will revolutionize the way you clean your shower or chop your veggies or slenderize your unsightly belly fat. But in the digital age, the concept has gone viral. Dozens, if not hundreds, of next-big-things are seemingly heralded every day in tweets, Facebook updates, and BuzzFeed listicles… and are just as promptly forgotten.

Humankind's sense of time has not always been so manically compressed or our craving of novelty so insatiable. But even in history's most static and tradition-bound moments, there have still been disruptive innovations that change the way we think and live. Even without media hype, there have been and always will be next big things.

This book is an attempt to describe some of history's next-big-things, the ideas and inventions that made possible the future that became us, and perhaps to suggest outlines of the future we are bequeathing to generations to follow.

This is of course a ridiculously ambitious goal. Even confining myself, as I have, to the last 3,000 years (more or less) and to the regions of the globe west of the Caucasus and north of Florida (more or less), I cannot remotely suggest that the list is complete. While I have tried to be fair to all my subjects, I don't claim to be objective: To identify innovations that have indelibly marked the present requires having a point of view about what the present is. Mine might diverge from yours. If that's the case, then consider this a provocation to hone your own counter interpretation. After all, I'm just this guy.

In applying the next-big-thing concept to the history of Western civilization, I've taken a philosophical turn. After pondering the idea over months of research and writing, I have come to think of a next-big-thing as a bet society makes on tomorrow. It's a nodal point in time, when the sprawl of history suddenly becomes still and clear, and we finally believe that we really know what the future is going to look like — because we have it here, in one convenient package. And we say with certainty, "*This will change everything.*"

But it's just a bet. For every idea, like philosophy, or invention, like the iPhone, that really does seem to change everything, there's a Segway that changes absolutely nothing.

To help make my case clear from the outset, I start each entry with an overview of its claim to fame (or infamy) and assign it ratings in two dimensions: the *hype factor*, which indicates the enthusiasm it generated at the time of its origin, and the *impact factor*, which is the more sober judgment of history.

Each entry is self-contained, so you can jump around wherever you like. However, themes do emerge, and there are cross-references if you'd like to follow them up.

So, what are you waiting for? Don't let the next big thing get away!

— **RICHARD FAULK**

ALCOHOL

"To alcohol! The cause of, and solution to, all of life's problems!"

TIME OF ORIGIN: *The mid-Proterozoic Era*

ORIGIN IN: *Fruit forests*

HYPE FACTOR: *0 — It's so old that when it first appeared, there was nothing to hype it.*

IMPACT FACTOR: *10 — Alcohol has been mankind's constant companion. It's embedded in our religious and social rituals; it's an art form, an industry, a pleasure, and a social blight. It's hard to imagine life without it.*

Life is hard and booze is fun. Poets and philosophers have been expounding on these sentiments from the beginning of recorded time. Next to having sex and breathing oxygen, finding solace and sustenance in alcohol might be the original next big thing.

In fact, it might even be older than that. If the hypothesis of some biologists is true, our taste for booze is so primordial that it might actually predate our existence as a species.

LET THERE BE BOOZE

Step back, if you will, to the oxygen-free, volcano-ridden, radiation-blasted hellscape that was the Earth some 3.5 billion years ago. Floating in the rich chemical soup of the primordial ocean (perhaps near some superheated vent on the deep-sea floor), some primitive, single-celled organisms are eagerly gobbling up simple sugars and expelling a frothy mix of carbon dioxide and ethanol. That's glycolysis — sugar fermentation — in action,

WHAT'S YOUR POISON?

Arguably alcohol's greatest success story is wine made from cultivated grapes. From earliest antiquity, it was a prestige beverage, the drink of gods and emperors, an indispensable part of religious and social solemnities. Even today, in the era of craft beers and resurrected cocktail sophistication, wine still owns pride of place. With a global production of 50 billion gallons a year compared to wine's seven billion, beer is still the crowd-pleaser, but wine retains the highest snob quotient.

Wine as we know it probably had its origin in eastern Turkey or the Caucasus. Gradually it moved down to the shores of the eastern Mediterranean, where the Phoenicians (the world's first great maritime traders) became major wine makers and exporters. Whereas beer spoils quickly, well-made and well-stored wine doesn't just last, it actually improves with age. This gave wine tremendous value as a commodity, and consumers across the known world became seduced by its flavor and exoticism.

Having hooked the Egyptian pharaohs on the novel beverage, the Phoenicians went on to sell them grape vines and, presumably, technical know-how via master vintners. From Egypt, wine appreciation spread to Greece, Italy, Spain, then France, and finally Northern Europe. And everywhere it went, wine displaced the local beverage to become the favored drink of the elite.

Not that the categories of alcohol were that clear-cut before the modern era. Scientist and alcohol historian Patrick McGovern believes that blended drinks, like the grog unearthed from Jianhu, were common in the early days of intentional fermentation. Until Roman times, it was common to flavor wine with infusions of herbs, honey, smoke, or resins. Today's vermouths are made via a process that's direct descendent from this practice, and distilled aperitifs, such as Campari and Chartreuse, are high-proof cousins.

and it's a process that's almost as old as life itself.

But the alcohol era really begins 100 million years ago, with the emergence of fruiting plants. Sweet and colorfully eye-catching, fruit practically calls out to energy-starved foragers, including, possibly, our earliest mammal ancestors (which somewhat resembled today's ferret). This ingenious seed-delivery system is all part of nature's tit for tat: The plants provide delicious calories, and, one way or another (if you catch my drift), the fruit eaters then disseminate the plant seeds.

Microorganisms also play a role in this game of symbiosis. Bursting overripe fruit is immediately set upon by wild yeasts that live on the fruit's skin, waiting for their chance to get into the sweet interior. The volatile alcohol excreted by the yeasts carries the fruit scent farther, advertising a rich and abundant energy source that's about to disappear. Happy memories of alcohol's euphoric effect encourages fruit eaters (a.k.a. frugivores) to work all the harder to seek out lightly spoiling fruit wherever they can find it, and the drug's effect as an appetite stimulant allows them to gorge all the more when they do.

The fermentation process, then, is just a part of Mother Nature's way of economizing: She'd be most unhappy if all that useful sugar went to waste.

Sound implausible that animals should be genetically driven to drink? Then try to explain why it is that, from fruit flies and slugs all the way to elephants, there is an alcohol-loving animal at every scale. Humans are far from the only creature that enjoys a tipple. Many of our primate cousins — chimpanzees, bonobos, howler monkeys, tree shrews — will drink when given the chance. Indeed, Darwin himself captured baboons by getting them helplessly drunk on beer.

And while we can't say definitively what other animals are subjectively experiencing, they do display the effects of drunkenness — unsteady walking/flying, drowsiness, and excited activity followed by a crash.

Which isn't to say that all creatures drink alike. In the lab, chimpanzees have been observed to guzzle about the equivalent of three or four bottles of wine before settling down to ride their buzz. On the other hand, rats prefer a more civilized predinner cocktail, followed up by a nightcap (although they also tend to congregate for a bender once or twice a week). Suburb-dwelling birds have it hard. Intoxicated from the contents of fruit trees and berry bushes in home gardens, they are prone to crashing into windows and sliding doors, the avian equivalent of a DUI.

HOMO BIBENS: DRINKING MAN

No one knows when we humans first realized that we didn't have to wait for fermentation to happen on its own, that we could control the process and shape the final product until it was stronger and more palatable than anything found in the wild. Because there is so little physical evidence of our earliest days, this question will probably remain unanswered. Any gourds, wooden cups, or leather flasks that might have held the very first home brews rotted away centuries ago.

The oldest known alcohol is a residue scraped off a clay pot that was fired in Jianhu, China, around the year 7000 BCE. Liquid chromatography-mass spectrometry indicates that the drink was made from a blend of fermented wild grapes and hawthorn berries bolstered with honey mead and rice wine. It probably had an alcohol content of 9 or 10 percent, about the same as a light white wine from today.

You can make booze out of anything that has a sufficient amount of sugar or starch: honey, wheat, barley, rice, corn, figs, dates, cassava, coconuts, grapes, berries, tree sap — even horse milk. And if you *can* do it, you can bet that at some time, in some place, people *have* done it. There's no universal progression in alcohol production. People just fermented whatever was most available. In Europe, for instance, that meant honey, which when fermented became mead, a drink that was celebrated in folktales and romances all the way down through the Middle Ages. In Ancient Egypt and the Middle East, the native drink was wine made from dates, palm, or figs. Technologically more difficult to make, grain-brewed beer nevertheless seems to have been a staple most anywhere grains were cultivated — in other words, nearly everywhere.

WE DRINK, THEREFORE WE ARE?

It's impossible to talk about alcohol without mentioning alcoholism or the violence, dysfunction, and self-harm that can result from drinking. But the very prevalence of alcoholism and binge drinking suggests to some scientists how ancient and deep-seated our relationship to alcohol is: It's stamped into our behavior, coded into our genetics.

And there are some benefits as well. Evolutionary psychologists suggest that getting a little drunk can moderate our herd instincts, which — despite their benefit to our species collectively — can lead us individually toward dullness and conformity. In the artificial sanctuary of our cities, survival instincts developed in the wild can misfire, causing depression and anxiety — which mild alcohol intake can offset. Some theorists go farther and say that our most human qualities — our impulse toward innovation, exploration, and imagination, our capacity for art and for religious experience — may have been aided by our relationship with alcohol. ●

THE CHARIOT

"And, as the seventh time now
The course was circled, on the Libyan car
Dashed their wild fronts: then order changed to ruin:
Car crashed on car; the wide Crissæan plain
Was sea-like strewed with wrecks; the Athenian saw,
Slackened his speed, and wheeling round the marge,
Unscathed and skillful, in the midmost space,
Left the wild tumult of that tossing storm."

— SOPHOCLES DESCRIBING A CHARIOT
RACE IN THE PLAY *ELECTRA*, 410 BCE

TIME OF ORIGIN: *Around 2100 BCE*

ORIGIN IN: *The plains between the eastern Urals and western Kazakhstan*

HYPE FACTOR: *8 — Its psychological impact was so profound that the chariot became a symbol of power and prestige for more than 2,000 years.*

IMPACT FACTOR: *8 — The chariot ruled the battlefield for a thousand years, and, as a sport, chariot racing endured for more than another thousand.*

The chariot is often considered the tank of the ancient world, but that's the wrong image. Light and maneuverable, the chariot was the first vehicle designed solely for speed. Picture instead a fleet of weaponized Ferraris — deadly, fast, and impossibly stylish.

BREAKING OUT OF THE (WAGON) RUT

The wheel is *the* iconic invention. Next to sliced bread, nothing else is more often evoked as a symbol of human ingenuity. But there's no evidence that the first appearance of a fine, handcrafted, artisanal wheel was greeted with any particular enthusiasm. Sure, it was *useful* — but where was the *wow* factor? Like those other basic machines, the lever and the inclined plane, the wheel simply isn't sexy.

Neither is the wagon, which, drawn by a pair of oxen or a now-extinct race of ass called the *onager*, was the world's oldest wheeled vehicle. At least, it's the oldest vehicle for which we have any evidence. The earliest evidence for the humble wagon appears around 3500 BCE, more or less simultaneously in a handful of sites throughout Central Europe and Mesopotamia. This is one invention that doesn't properly belong to the Chinese; they had to wait nearly 1,500 years before they got wagons of their own.

Unspectacular as it is, a wagon is nevertheless a pretty refined piece of technology. In addition to the wheels, you need axles that are strong enough to bear the weight of the body but thin enough that they don't cause too much drag. Then you need a harness to connect the draft team to the cart — preferably one that fits over the shoulders rather than the throat, so the oxen don't choke themselves as they pull — and you need something to steer with. Originally, this was a ring through the animal's nose with a rope tied to it. And finally, it helps to have a system of good roads — after all, if your path is too bumpy or too muddy or too sandy or too steep or too windy, your wagon is apt to break or get stuck. (Just ask the American pioneers who attempted to "go West" using wagon power.) It's no wonder that the Native Americans abstained from wheeled travel and opted instead for sledges or just going on foot!

Creaking and plodding, the wagon was the stolid delivery van of antiquity. Then one day, the first chariot came careening through the fields of the Fertile Crescent at breakneck speed — clattering, rumbling, and pursued by a cloud of dust that would never overtake it. And the world understood what it was to love a machine.

As soon as the chariot (and the chariot army) arrived on the scene, every emperor, tyrant, and god-king from Akkad to Uruk simply had to have his own. For 500 years, chariots would dominate the battlefield and decide the fate of dynasties. For another 2,000 years, legends of chariot-driving heroes would captivate listeners gathered around campfires and inside feasting halls everywhere from China to India and Persia, and on to Greece and Western Europe.

The chariot was a marvel of woodworking. Newly invented spoke wheels weighed just one tenth of conventional solid wheels, and the entire contraption was light enough for a man to carry. Subsequent refinements — which included lowering the number of spokes from eight down to four and replacing the solid floor with leather webbing that also acted as a shock absorber — shaved even more weight. No less revolutionary was the engine — the first to be measured in actual horsepower. Pulled by a team of two horses, the chariot was five times faster than the ox cart and could easily outpace even unharnessed donkeys.

REASSESSING THE CHARIOT'S ORIGINS

For many years scholars assumed that this breakthrough of design, carpentry, and animal husbandry must have been the product of the advanced, urban cultures of Mesopotamia. But they overlooked one detail: The people who best understood horses weren't living in the bustling cities of Babylon or Ur. They were uncouth seminomads to the north, living at the fringes of the known world. It was there, where the forests and mountains of eastern Europe meet the vast grassy steppe that rolls in unbroken from China, that the horse was first domesticated nearly 6,000 years ago. And it was there that the oldest chariot remains have now been found, excavated from warrior graves that were built in settlements just east of the Ural Mountains as far back 2100 BCE.

Archaeologists call these chariot builders the Sintashta, and there is compelling evidence that they might have spoken the earliest ancestor of Indo-European, a language family that includes Greek, Latin, Sanskrit, and almost every modern European tongue, including English. In other words, these wild people might have been real-life Aryans, the semi-mythical forebears of Western civilization. And the chariot almost certainly played a role in their spread.

No one really knows what warfare looked like in the ancient world. The documents are hard to interpret, and artistic depictions are conventionalized and often ambiguous. Archeological evidence suggests that the original chariot warriors probably shot arrows or flung javelins on the go. (If you stick a spear into someone from a moving chariot, you'll get knocked off your feet from the impact, so, sorry, there wasn't any chariot jousting.) The *Iliad* describes archaic Greek chariot warriors racing around the battlefield and then leaping off to engage in combat on foot. It's like a muscular version of speed dating, with participants scanning for the right partner to engage in a little heated mano-a-mano before dashing off to the next engagement. But since the *Iliad* was composed about 800 years after the events it describes, the representation is most likely how the Ancient Greeks, who mostly fought on foot, imagined that the even Ancient-er Greeks went to war.

However they fought exactly, chariot warriors were undeniably studly. It took formidable skill, balance, and strength to drive a chariot. Think about how tricky it is just to stand in a moving bus. While later chariots accommodated a two-person crew — one to drive and one to fight (and sometimes a third to hold up a shield) — the earliest versions may have been one-seaters. The driver would have held the reins with one hand while fighting with the other. An Egyptian carving shows a pharaoh steering with his hips while shooting arrows, which is an impractical but not an impossible way to fight. Nevertheless, Egyptian artists are infamous for portraying their kings doing fantastically cool things, so we shouldn't assume that the illustration depicts a literal truth.

THE GOLDEN AGE AND SLOW DECLINE

The golden age of chariot warfare began around 1700 BCE. In Crete and southern Greece, Indo-European speakers established powerful kingdoms backed up with the might of large chariot armies. They also built Troy on the western edge of modern-day Turkey and soon after began conquering northern India. In the more established regions of the Fertile Crescent,

Hattusilis I led a chariot army to become the first Hittite emperor. Meanwhile in Egypt, a mysterious chariot people called the Hyksos toppled the Pharaoh to establish the Fifteenth Dynasty.

The largest chariot battle was fought at Kadesh around 1275 BCE between the two superpowers of the day, the Hittites and the Egyptians. Although the propaganda of Pharaoh Ramses II counted it a major victory, the battle was probably a draw. But regardless of the outcome, it was a massive affair: Some 5,000 chariots took to the field to dispute Egypt's northern border.

More effective infantry and the emergence of cavalry (individually mounted warriors who could offer more maneuverability) made the chariot obsolete around 800 BCE. By the Classical Era, chariots had dwindled to just a nominal force in the Persian army. When Alexander the Great's army of cavalry and massed, spear-carrying infantry toppled the last Persian emperor in 331 BCE, the victory marked the end of the chariot as a significant military machine in the West. (That being said, it did endure on the battlefield for almost another thousand years among the Celts, and, especially, the Chinese.)

But the chariot went on to a second life as a sporting vehicle. Chariot racing was popular in the cities of Alexander the Great's empire, but it became an obsession in the Roman Empire and its later Byzantine incarnation. During the fourth century, Christianized Romans — particularly in the new capitol, Constantinople — started losing their taste for bloody gladiatorial games and turned for thrills to chariot racing instead. Like sports fans of today, supporters of the two major teams, the Greens and the Blues, wore their team colors. They even sported distinctive clothes and haircuts. They also sometimes engaged in acts of hooliganism that would put modern European soccer fans to shame: Contentious races could trigger sprees of murder, kidnap, rape, and arson. The Nika Revolt of 532, which nearly toppled the Emperor Justinian and left some 30,000 dead, was ignited by a chariot race.

After that point, interest in chariot racing started to decline. But, unlike gladiatorial contests and other pagan spectacles, the races were never banned by the Christian emperors. In 1204 CE, crusaders from Western Europe sacked Constantinople on their way to the Holy Land. Jousting was more to the taste of these new occupiers than chariot races. Although the empire would recover and struggle on for several more centuries, chariot racing did not come back — with the exception, perhaps, of the genteel sport of harness racing, which appeared in the nineteenth century. ●

PHILOSOPHY

"Gods of course did not reveal everything to mortals from the beginning, but in time by searching they improve their discoveries."

— XENOPHANES OF COLOPHON

TIME OF ORIGIN: *Early sixth century BCE*

ORIGIN IN: *Western Turkey*

HYPE FACTOR: *5 — The first philosophers didn't have a PR machine beyond their immediate disciples, and many of their neighbors regarded them merely as unemployed eccentrics.*

IMPACT FACTOR: *10 — Thinking about the universe in terms of matter and energy rather than supernatural activity was a major conceptual hurdle to clear.*

We live in hard times for the venerable institution of philosophy. In our data-driven, technocratic culture, deep contemplation of the human condition is scoffed at as a waste of processing power, its conclusions unquantifiable and hopelessly subjective. But wherever you fall on the humanities vs. STEM divide, it should be acknowledged that the fundamental philosophical intuition — that reality is rational and open to human understanding — is a far from self-evident insight that has become a cornerstone of our thinking.

THE PHYSIOLOGOI

When we think of the great cities of Ancient Greece, fifth-century-BCE Athens is probably the first to come to mind. At the close of the Persian Wars, this upstart center of a small and short-lived empire was much like the United States at the end of World War II. But just a few generations earlier, the pinnacle of Greek culture was far from Athens; it wasn't even in mainland Greece. That honor went to the wealthy and sophisticated colonies in Ionia, on the westward-facing coast of modern-day Turkey.

According to our scanty evidence, it was the Ionian city of Miletus where philosophical thought was born, right out of the head of a fellow named Thales, sometime around 600 BCE.

This claim, of course, begs the intensely philosophical question: *What is philosophy?*

As you were probably taught at some point, *philosophy* literally means "love of wisdom" — which, as you probably at thought the time, is a lousy definition for anything.

If we look at the very early philosophers, however, we'll see that they had a diverse skill set: According to legend, Thales introduced geometry to Egypt, predicted a solar eclipse, and once cornered the olive oil market — just to prove that a philosopher could actually get rich, if he wanted to; Thales' intellectual successor, Anaximander, reputedly invented the sundial and made the first map of the world. So clearly, for all their abstract thinking, these first philosophers were practical men who were deeply and rigorously interested in the physical world. They wanted to know what reality was and where it all came from.

This is probably what Aristotle had in mind when he called Thales and his successors *physiologoi*, or "naturalists." Buried in Aristotle's term, though, is a root that gives us more precise guidance: *logos*, that most elusively Greek of Greek words. *Logos* means many things, but uniting all its definitions is the idea of reason or logical ordering. The Ionian "physiologues" were obsessed with *logos*.

For them, the universe was a *cosmos*, an *arrangement* with an intelligible logic. The revolutionary idea behind philosophy is that the universe is self-ordering, a process of perpetual growth and change that obeys inherent principles of organization. It wasn't the plaything of the gods, as it was in the religious poems of Hesiod and Homer.

Through observation and reflection, the philosophers of Miletus sought to discover the original source of matter. Thales decided it was water; Anaximenes, the last in this tradition, countered that it was air; Anaximander, who came in between them, argued that it was just undifferentiated "stuff." Whatever their disagreements, all three thinkers shared the same assumption: Reason alone was sufficient to explain everything. You didn't need to invoke the gods or resort to other metaphysical interventions. *Logos* reigned supreme.

In postulating that the universe could be understood solely through natural phenomena, Thales and his successors were as much the first scientists as they were the first philosophers. But they weren't entirely mechanistic. They saw in the logical ordering of the cosmos, in its infinite balancing of forces and counterforces, the expression of a principle that in human interaction is called *justice*. Morality itself was inherent in the order of the universe.

Miletus wasn't the only Greek city noted for its philosophers. The new thinking spread throughout Ionia and to the Greek colonies in southern Italy, too. Individual philosophers followed their own interests, borrowed freely, and rejected equally freely the theories of their peers. So, while they all understood that they were engaged in the same intellectual project, it's impossible to generalize their ideas.

THE SOPHISTS

As high civilization came to mainland Greece, life for the average citizen became more complex. Knowing how to read, count, and fight no longer comprised a sufficient education for a gentleman. To meet this demand for knowledge, a new breed of philosopher-educator appeared: the sophist. Although they could talk cosmology, sophists earned their living by teaching more practical skills — or at least skills that were considered practical in the ancient world: oratory, literary analysis, morals, and political science.

Citizenship in the world of the Greek city-states was an exclusive privilege that was extended only to wealthy, land-owning males. Its two great responsibilities were to fight for the city when necessary and to govern it. Consequently, rhetorical skill — the power to inspire men on the battlefield and to persuade them in political debate — was most highly prized.

Because of their focus on rhetoric and their ability to argue any side of an argument, the sophists were caricatured as being amoral and self-serving, much as we caricature lawyers today. To this day, as a general term, *sophist* refers to someone who manipulates logic for their own advantage.

PHILOSOPHY, YEAR ZERO

Socrates, the most famous of philosophers, had a low opinion of sophists and their instrumental use of logic. Instead, he defined philosophy as the search for what was truthful rather than merely useful. In doing this, Socrates put philosophy on the course we recognize today. In most accounts, then, philosophy really begins around the year 390 BCE, when his disciple, Plato, started documenting Socrates' conversations and debates. For this reason, despite their considerable differences, earlier philosophers are generically called *the pre-Socratics*.

In his search for the truth, Socrates developed a method of relentless questioning that would ultimately maneuver his intellectual adversaries into expressing an irreconcilable contradiction, an unsupportable premise, or an outright admission of ignorance. This is the *elenctic* or *Socratic method*. It's also known as the *why-mom-why-mom-why-mom?* style of inquiry.

A self-proclaimed gadfly, Socrates would have been an annoyance even at the best of times. But Athens in 399 BCE was engaged in a major war with Sparta. Socrates' philosophical questioning was seen as unpatriotic and undermining of traditional values. Accused of impiety and of corrupting the young, Socrates was convicted and sentenced to death.

The goal was probably just to get him to shut up and leave the city. But, true to his nature, Socrates stayed and insisted that the brutal sentence be carried out. As a result, his death became a historic example of the importance of dissent and intellectual freedom, even in times of national crisis.

Who said philosophers couldn't be hardcore? •

RELIGION AS PERSONAL FAITH

"I cannot be called anything other than what I am — a Christian."

— VIBIA PERPETUA, THIRD-CENTURY ROMAN ARISTOCRAT, CHRISTIAN MARTYR, AND SAINT

TIME OF ORIGIN: *Second and third centuries of the Common Era*

ORIGIN IN: *Roman Empire*

HYPE FACTOR: *10 — Not only were the lives of the martyrs meticulously recorded and voraciously read by the pious — as they still are today — but the acrimonious and often public debates between pagans and Christians were widely enjoyed by partisans on both sides.*

IMPACT FACTOR: *10 — This relationship with the divine is enshrined in today's three dominant monotheistic religions.*

That simple statement of faith uttered by an early martyr expresses a radicalism that we moderns can barely perceive.

For those of us accustomed to thinking of religion within the terms set by the Abrahamic faiths — Judaism, Christianity, and Islam — faith is the cornerstone. Without sincere belief, a person's religious devotion is suspect, less than perfect. We assume that religion isn't inherited in quite the same way that we inherit the rest of our cultural legacy, but that it's also a personal choice, an affirmative commitment that says something profound about our individual identity. We expect our deity to make demands not just regarding our public behavior but, even more importantly, regarding our most private thoughts and desires.

In the ancient world, this intrusion into the cramped spaces of the mere mortal soul would have seemed bizarre and disgracefully petty — even for divinities as infamously capricious and jealous as the Olympian gods.

Why exactly the citizens of the Roman Empire decided to throw over their traditional gods for a breakaway Jewish sect that embraced a belief set so radically unlike religion as they had known it for a thousand years is a question that defies any simple answer. What can be shown, however, is the enormity of the spiritual and historical watershed that was reached in 313, when the emperor Constantine the Great officially sanctioned Christianity, making it all but in name the official religion of the Roman people.

THAT (ORIGINAL) OLD-TIME RELIGION

In Ancient Greece and Rome, the traditional job of religion was more to foster social cohesion than to provide individual spiritual fulfillment. Communities came together to sacrifice and feast in honor of the gods — and the gods, in turn, would deliver good weather, abundant crops, and victory in battle. This exchange of favors mirrored the mafia-like political life of the poleis and provinces, where wealthy and influential patrons received the support of those below them in exchange for jobs, gifts, or the promise of a favorable hearing at a legal trial.

Intangibles like faith, conscience, or the hope for eternal life after death had no place in this moral universe. The gods didn't care whether you believed in them. They cared even less whether you approved of them. What they cared about was respect. As long as the sacrifices kept coming, you were A-OK. But if you forgot, God help you.

The ancient notion of piety was closely associated with family honor and civic pride. Within every respectable Roman household was an altar sanctified to departed ancestors, and displays of filial piety were an essential part of well-bred behavior. (As with the gods, it was important to keep

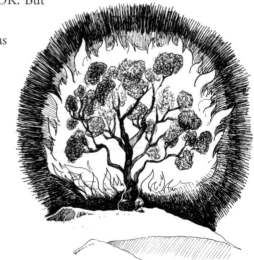

the dead happy, or they might take it out against you, from beyond the grave.) In the public sphere, ostentatious sacrifices and expensive public works, such as the commissioning of statues and the restoring of temples, became a way for local elites to compete for social prestige — an early example of doing well by doing good.

To look at the subject from a sociological point of view, traditional worship of the Olympian gods fulfilled a stabilizing function in the community by joining all levels of civic life in collective worship and channeling the potentially destructive ambition of the powerful into displays that benefited the whole community and blurred otherwise stark social inequalities.

SPIRITUAL SEEKERS?

But there was another side to ancient religion: the mystery cults. These were secretive associations with restricted membership, the oldest and most famous of which were the Eleusinian Mysteries, which were celebrated near ancient Athens and honored Demeter, goddess of agriculture and fertility.

No one ever "converted" to Zeus worship; it was just something you participated in as an upstanding member of your community — sort of the same way you don't have to be American or even particularly patriotic to enjoy a Fourth of July firework display and picnic. The mystery cults, on the other hand, required personal commitment in the form of an initiation rite. About the specifics of these rites we know very little, but apparently they could sometimes be quite harrowing, perhaps involving the simulated death of the initiate or a ritualistic enactment of the killing of the god.

In fact, we don't know much about mystery cults at all. Very little surviving literature discusses them, and much of what does was written by disapproving Christians. The original meaning of *mystēs* is "an initiate," but so complete was the secrecy shrouding these cults that the word came to mean "something puzzling and inexplicable," as it does today.

Generally speaking, though, mystery cults seemed to have been associated with agriculture and sexuality — their practices may even have included drug-inspired orgies tied to the cycle of the seasons. (On the other hand, the *galli*, priests of the mother goddess Cybele, were expected to castrate themselves in her honor — so you had to pick your cult with care.) But the orgies might have been nothing more than nasty propaganda; it's hard to tell. It's more certain, however, that the cults promised liberation from the fear of death — perhaps in the form of life after death, but more likely via a spiritual rebirth in the here and now, or maybe just in a reassuring vision of life as an eternal cycle of birth, death, and rebirth.

While at least some mystery cults offered something we might call spiritual redemption, we would probably regard them as something between a social club and a religion proper. They offered no theology to speak of and no grand theory of the cosmos or our place in it. Likewise, they made no demands on the faith of their initiates. There was no credo, no dogma. Since there were examples of child-priests inducted into multiple cults, it's clear that for at least some mystery cults there could have been few teachings to learn and no official functions to perform.

If you're looking for lively sectarian debate in antiquity on the purpose and nature of life, you'd have to turn not to religion but to philosophy. Among the philosophical schools there was fierce — sometimes violent — partisanship. Platonists and Aristotelians, Epicureans and stoics, Pythagoreans and cynics might loudly accuse each other of being fundamentally deluded about the nature of reality. But in religion, all was ease and amity: There was always room for another god, always space for more ritual.

Superficial as they may seem against our standards of piety, mystery cults were extraordinarily popular during the height and early decline of the Roman Empire. For the first two centuries of the Common Era, people at every level of society — emperors and slaves, citizens and noncitizens, male, and, for the most part, female — participated in cultic worship.

Perhaps this vogue showed that there was a hunger for a more personally meaningful spirituality. Of course the evidence is scant, and the question itself is one that these possible spiritual seekers might not have understood. But we do know that in the second and third century people flocked to a strange new Eastern cult, one that would eventually sweep the empire, radically altering the relations between divinity and humankind and sidelining easygoing religious toleration for almost 2,000 years.

THE COMMUNITY OF GOD

When historians attempt to explain the spread of Christianity throughout the Roman Empire, they point to the turmoil of the third century, when 200 years of Roman-enforced peace erupted into a century of civil war, with all its attendant instability.

Old values were decaying and traditional public religion was languishing in this new age of violence and naked ambition. As conspicuous displays of private wealth and power lost their power to offend good taste, the wealthy stopped funding temples to the gods and started building palaces for themselves instead. Community bonds were forged now in arenas and hippodromes, where cheering factions rallied behind hero athletes.

More than ever before, people were on the move, leaving the countryside for the protection of cities, or trading in meager hometown prospects for opportunities in distant lands. With fewer connections to draw upon, these newly dislocated individuals were often drawn to the community offered by Christianity, a fellowship where ethnicity and social class didn't matter and where love and charity were mandated by divine precept.

Throughout centuries of subjugation and dispersal, Jews had known these sustaining bonds of community and religion. Their sense of separateness, of a special relationship with their god, had preserved Jewish identity despite considerable pressure to assimilate with conquering Babylonians, Persians, Greeks, and Romans. But Judaism was an exclusive club. Membership came only through birth.

Early on, however, the followers of the rabbi Jesus opened their community to anyone with sincere intent. In the Greek-speaking world of the early Christians, the word for *church* was *ekklesia*, which at the time meant "a civic assembly." With no other metaphors in their cultural lexicon to describe the profound feeling of community and commitment these Greco-Roman believers were experiencing, they used language of citizenship.

When St. Perpetua declared herself a Christian — a declaration that would promptly deliver her into the jaws of a hungry lion — she was professing her new citizenship in a community that was challenging fundamental ideas of Romanness. This new mystery cult promised absolute support for coreligionists but demanded it as well. Jesus had preached that it was possible to serve God as a Christian and Caesar as a citizen — but as a Christian, it was impossible to worship Caesar. No more live and let live: This new jealous god would tolerate no peaceable coexistence with other deities.

For the early Christians, then, as for no Romans before them, the choice of religion was a profound revelation of personal faith and devotion. For good and for ill, it went to the core of their individual beings in a way that traditional religion never had and was never meant to.

"FOR GOD SO LOVED THE WORLD..."

Greco-Roman culture was never gentle. It was a winner-take-all society that prized strength and energy, and didn't think so much about mercy or charity. The original Olympic games, for instance, awarded no silver or bronze prizes: There was only one winner... and a bunch of losers — who were sometimes lucky just to escape with their lives.

For those who felt the brunt of the especially aggressive and ambitious early centuries of the Common Era — slaves, poor urban workers, skilled laborers struggling to hold onto what little they had — the idea of an omnipotent god, who, as a sign of compassion and love, manifested himself as an obscure peasant and allowed himself to endure the humiliation of injustice and the agony of death, was extraordinarily powerful. No Olympian had ever demonstrated such a kinship with the world and the creatures that populated it.

Humility in the face of the boundless mysteries that engulf us, and an obligation to aid those who grope their way alongside us — these ideas were not necessarily unique to Christianity, but they were certainly alien to the prevailing Roman outlook. To embrace them as imperatives was a seismic shift in moral thought. Balanced against the call to humility, however, was an ennobling idea — that we were each crafted in the image of a loving God. Every human life had value.

While these spiritual values may have been more revered than adhered to, it's easy to see their appeal and to understand how they could have spread so quickly and endured for so long. ●

THE FLYING BUTTRESS

"The principle of the Gothic architecture is Infinity made imaginable."

— SAMUEL TAYLOR COLERIDGE, 1833

TIME OF ORIGIN: *c. 1170*

ORIGIN IN: *France*

HYPE FACTOR: *2 — Medieval culture was highly conservative in outlook and reluctant to hype novelties.*

IMPACT FACTOR: *4 — Enabled by the flying buttress, Gothic architecture flourished for 300 years and was the first European style to free itself from classical influence.*

We don't generally think of the Middle Ages as a period of technological activity. But from windmills and waterwheels to crossbows and the introduction of gunpowder, there was plenty of technology in use. The Middle Ages was also a period of intensive building. Wooden forts were replaced by stone castles, churches were restored, cathedrals founded, civic buildings and guild halls erected. And in the midst of this construction boom, builders were innovating what would be called the Gothic architecture, the first distinctly European style to emerge as the Western world started to free itself from the influence of the old Roman Empire.

With its distinctly pointed arches and spires that soared well beyond those of any buildings before and seemed to reach out to God himself, Gothic architecture was a wonder of engineering. Essential to Gothic architecture was a technical innovation called *the flying buttress*.

A EUROPEAN ARCHITECTURE

Height and delicacy: These were the supreme concerns of the architect. How could they build taller, lighter walls that would not buckle and collapse?

Heavy arched stone ceilings push not just downward but outward. To counter that thrust, walls traditionally had to be thick and solid, admitting just small windows. But beginning in about 1100, architects started innovating. They discovered that pointed arches deliver less lateral thrust than round arches. They also found ways of removing stress from outer walls by using pillars to help support ceilings. Finally, they discovered the flying buttress. Resembling a half-arch leaning against a wall from the outside, this form of buttress connects a heavy vertical base to a wall by means of a bridge-like support called a *flyer*.

Set at regular intervals, these reinforcements allowed architects to strip walls down to mere skeletons. Despite their towering size, Gothic buildings were flooded with light from the many windows that could now be set in. Filtered through stained glass designs that became marvelously developed in this era, the light conveyed a wonderful and mysterious otherworldly feel.

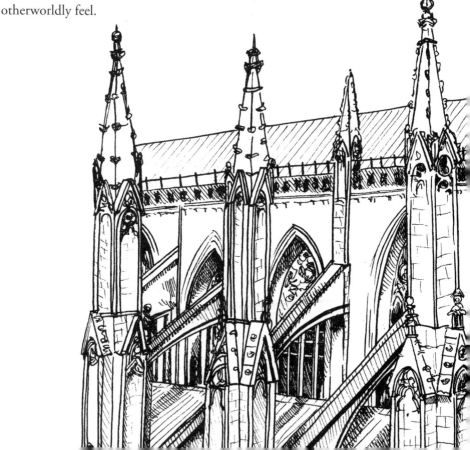

A STYLE WITH NO NAME

Starting in Paris, Gothic architecture gradually spread as far as Croatia in the east, up into England, and even down to Italy. It was the dominant style for 300 years.

And yet, it didn't have a name. Chroniclers often referred to as *the modern style* or *the French style*. The term *Gothic* wasn't coined until 1550, by the Florentine artist-historian Giorgio Vasari. He meant it as an insult.

Vasari was a committed classicist who saw the ancient civilizations of Greece and Rome as having set the standard for all human achievement. He was the first person to use the term *Renaissance*. To Vasari, the spiky arches, lurid colored light, and disproportionate features of the modern style were barbaric, a travesty of good taste, and a betrayal of classical values. Contemptuously, he named the style *Gothic* after one of the barbarian tribes that overran the Roman Empire.

This dim view of Gothic architecture lingered into the eighteenth century. But eventually connoisseurs warmed up to it again, and there was even a Gothic revival in the nineteenth century. Although it has long since lost its negative connotations, the term *Gothic* remains. ●

SINGLE-POINT PERSPECTIVE

"Oh, what a lovely thing this perspective is!"

— FIFTEENTH-CENTURY PERSPECTIVE
PIONEER PAOLO UCCELLO, REPLYING
TO HIS WIFE'S ENTREATIES TO QUIT
WORKING AND COME TO BED ALREADY

TIME OF ORIGIN: *Early fifteenth century*

ORIGIN IN: *Florence, Italy*

HYPE FACTOR: *8 — After a hugely influential author made the case that perspective constituted a triumph for the modern world over the ancient world, perspective became the emblem of the Renaissance.*

IMPACT FACTOR: *8 — Beyond simply being a cool new illusionistic technique, perspective made ripples beyond the art world by putting an unprecedented emphasis on subjective perception.*

If you think of the Renaissance as the dawn of humanism and the rebirth of interest in classical authors, then the Renaissance starts in the mid-fourteenth century with the Italian poets Petrarch and Boccaccio.

But who thinks of it that way?

For most of us the Renaissance is all about the art. It's something you can see, in sculpture, architecture, and, especially, in painting. Where else is the sprit of that age more immediately present than in the scintillating colors of newly popularized oil paint; in the artistic focus on realistic detail, human anatomy, and individual expressiveness; and, not least of all, in the illusionistic treatment of space, made possible by the discovery of linear perspective?

Leon Battista Alberti, a serious contender for the title of First Renaissance Man Ever, felt the same way. In fact, he was so excited by the new artwork being produced by painters in early fifteenth-century Florence that he wrote a book to introduce them to the larger art world and to popularize their techniques among patrons and other artists throughout Italy.

Published in 1436, Alberti's *On Painting* presents the first systematic explanation of linear perspective — a geometric riddle that, once solved, became the cornerstone of painting in the Renaissance and for another 500 years to follow. Influencing the theory and practice of every other Renaissance artist you've ever heard of, including Leonardo da Vinci, *On Painting* was so heavily consulted that, in the words of one Alberti translator, the Italian version was "read out of existence." In 1600, a whole new edition had to be started from scratch.

Perspective, like realism in general, may no longer be an essential part of our aesthetic enjoyment of a painting, but the book that introduced it is still of interest for another innovation: It is one of the first books to elevate the artist from the status of craft worker to that of creative genius.

RECOGNIZING THE RENAISSANCE

Leon Alberti is today remembered primarily as an architect and an art theorist, but he was also, among other things, a priest, a lawyer, an athlete, a playwright, a poet, an orator, an academic, a mathematician, a papal secretary, a classicist, a painter, and a sculptor. But even this textbook Renaissance man did not fully appreciate that he was living in a new era of history until he visited Florence in 1434 and saw the art.

In Alberti's estimation, the current batch of Florentine artists were so bold in innovation and so well skilled in technique that they not only rivaled the masters of antiquity, they surpassed them. It was as though he were living through a moment of cultural — what might one call it? — *rebirth...?*

One feature in particular of the new art so struck Alberti that he described it as the "greatest work of the painter." This was a dramatic and immersive style of composition that Alberti named *istoria*. The subject of a well articulated *istoria* was instantly understandable to any audience, no matter how refined or ignorant, and the style was characterized by at least one framing figure — an angel or a shepherd, maybe, someone on the edges of the story, who acknowledged the viewer's presence in an unprecedentedly vivid and personal way, inviting them in with a gaze or a gesture.

The linchpin of the *istoria* was a geometrical system that allowed the artist to depict in the painting a visual space that blended seamlessly into the viewer's. Alberti named this *prospettiva*; today we know it as *single-point perspective*.

RATIONALIZING SPACE

Imagine a street retreating out of sight, straight into the distance. The edges of the street appear to converge until they meet in a single point, when they vanish on the horizon. The horizon corresponds with the eye level of the viewer, and the vanishing point of the road aligns directly with the viewer's eye.

There's no way you didn't already know that. And that's why Alberti's idea remains one of the most influential of all time.

Once an artist establishes the vanishing point on a canvas, he or she can draft a scene that looks convincingly illusionistic to anyone standing exactly opposite that point. Astute observers have recognized this phenomenon for as long as we've had eyes to see with, but the first to tackle it systematically as an artistic and mathematical challenge were Florentine artists half a generation older than Alberti.

Finding the geometry to accurately simulate the third dimension is not as easy as it might seem. Representing receding straight lines is a snap, but circles and spheres are tough. Moreover, three-dimensional objects don't just narrow from side to side as they recede; they also grow shallower. Representing that contraction consistently is also tricky.

The first artists to use perspective derived their own systems, which were like trade secrets. With surprising generosity, however, Alberti published his — not to make money but because he was a true evangelist of the new painting style. It was his aim to raise the standard of art and to cultivate informed viewers and patrons who could fully understand and appreciate it.

The word *perspective* comes from the Latin for "look though," and for Alberti, that's exactly what it allowed an artist to do. A picture surface, for him, was like an imaginary window — which is not an obvious premise, if you think about it. It might have made more sense for Alberti to think in terms of projecting a three-dimensional image onto a flat surface, which is closer to what a painter is actually doing. Instead, he wrote as though the picture surface were indeed transparent and the artist rendering an actual scene on the other side of it.

The way Alberti wrote about perspective shows his debt to the science of optics. And it shows that Alberti was thinking about more than just art. For him, the perspective system was not a mathematical trick or a technical cheat to ease the job of the professional painter. It was real. It was an accurate description of how vision works and the reflection a physical truth — namely that even empty space has an order; that, in a sense, it is not empty at all. Rather — like the X, Y, Z grid we study in geometry class — it is infinitely replete with points that articulate the relationship between objects and make the world a coherent whole, not a hodgepodge of fragmented matter. [See **Magnetic Philosophy** for another example of how empirical models of space were being justified — and resisted — at about this time.]

Conceptually, this was a major break with the medieval approach to painting, which was still thriving in northern Europe and other parts of Italy.

REPRESENTING THE UNREPRESENTABLE

Medieval painters thought of themselves as craftspeople employing technique, not creative artists attempting personal expression or realistic representation. Like the Ancient Egyptian artisans before them, they worked within narrow conventions (though not quite *that* narrow), and the purpose of their artwork was primarily didactic — to make vivid familiar stories from the Bible, to convey the piety and awe of the saints, to render more tangible the ineffable power of the divine.

Because the art was all about ideas, it didn't need to be particularly realistic, not much more than the word *dog* needs to look like an actual dog. A church fresco was there to remind you of cosmic truths that transcended words and images — the redemptive suffering of Christ, the resolute serenity of the Virgin Mary, or the boundless majesty to God — not to fool you into thinking that your were looking through a window onto the street outside.

Not that realistic representation was utterly neglected. To help on that front, medieval painters possessed tools of the trade that were not too different in principle from Alberti's perspective system. They memorized schemes that defined the proportions of the face in terms of nose lengths and used the size of the head to control for the height and width of the body. There is even one enigmatic but suggestive manual from the 1200s that might indicate that medieval artists worked up realistic sketches from basic geometrical forms — like those children's drawing books from today that show you how to cartoon a crocodile or a lion's face out of superimposed triangles, rectangles, and circles.

But painters on either side of the cultural watershed that split the fifteenth century approached their systems from opposite directions. As one eminent art historian has quipped, the purpose of art theory in the Renaissance was "to aid the artist in coming to terms with reality on an observational basis," while in the Middle Ages it was all about saving the artist "the trouble of direct observation of reality." (It's probably wittier in the original German.)

THE BIRTH OF GENIUS

Like many disruptive technologies, single-point perspective was in some respects a step backward. Instead of making painters more efficient and productive, as the medieval proportions systems had, it slowed them down by imposing greater demands. A plausible picture space now had to be filled with plausible people. They should look as real and individual as the crowd in any piazza. They must be clad in the recognizable garments of their station and profession, and each individual must clearly show "the movements of his soul" — not stereotyped expressions, but the subtle presentation of recognizable psychology.

After Alberti, it was no longer sufficient for painters to know how to mix paint, prepare a painting surface, and sketch upon it. They had to be intellectuals now, both mathematicians and students of human nature. Alberti had promoted the artist from tradesman to gentleman and a liberal artist. With great judgment and a subtle understanding of the stories they were commissioned to represent, the artists of the Renaissance had to know how best to reinterpret their source texts, to know what elements to emphasize and what to discard so as to speak most directly and powerfully to the audience. If the challenge of the medieval painter was to render a God's-eye view, the Renaissance painter's obsession was with capturing humanity in its particularity.

"MANKIND, THE MEASURE OF ALL THINGS"

The above observation by the Greek philosopher Protagoras became the motto of the Renaissance humanists, who placed humankind at the center of the cosmos. This is not to say that they believed that humans are the greatest of all creations; they merely recognized that, since our own experience is the only thing we know with certainty, any attempt to understand the rest of the world must start from there.

Alberti used Protagoras's idea literally, by employing human proportions to organize the space of his artwork. As we've seen, the viewer's eye level defined the vanishing point; but it also corresponded with the eye level of the major figures on the canvas. Furthermore, Alberti recommended that before sketching, the artist lay out a preliminary grid using as a standard of measurement one-third the height of the people to be rendered.

But the human viewer outside the painting was also crucially important. Perspective can be thought of as a machine that works in two directions: On one hand, it enables an artist to construct a visually coherent vista, but, in doing so, it simultaneously creates a space outside the picture for its own optimal viewing — that is to say, the place where the artist stood while executing the scene. Without a viewer standing in just the right place, the painting is incomplete: The illusionistic perspective machine does not function.

By its very structure, then, painting put an unprecedented focus on the artist. Whatever the subject, it was always seen quite literally from the painter's point of view. Flat and stylized medieval art could be enjoyed equally well from multiple positions. But with the new perspective art, viewers were continually reminded that they were looking at a particular scene, from a certain angle, at a certain distance.

This emphasis on particular individuality subject sweeps European intellectual life starting in the Renaissance. It is in painting, philosophy, politics, literature, even the theology of the Reformation, which emphasized an individual relationship with the divine. It is also at the core of scientific revolution, which would ignite a century later.

Alberti's book, then, is on much more than painting. It's a foundational document for a worldview that we still share today. ●

THE MOVABLE TYPE PRINTING PRESS

"Everything that has been written to me about that remarkable man… is quite true. I did not see complete Bibles but sections… the text of which was absolutely free from error *and printed with extreme elegance and accuracy. Your Eminence would have read them with no difficulty and without the aid of spectacles…. I do not have any doubt about the* perfection of the volumes.*"*

— THE FUTURE POPE PIUS II ON MEETING
JOHANNES GUTENBERG, 1455

TIME OF ORIGIN: *About 1450*

ORIGIN IN: *Mainz, Germany*

HYPE FACTOR: *8 — It was much harder to get buzz going in early modern Europe, but printing press hype is still enduring.*

IMPACT FACTOR: *10 — This was the most significant innovation in communications since the book itself, maybe even since written language.*

No surprise here. The movable type printing press as developed by Johannes Gutenberg is invariably listed among the most influential inventions in the history of technology. But this isn't just modern hype. There is ample evidence that people of Gutenberg's day fully appreciated the revolutionary nature of the press.

JOHANNES GENSFLEISCH ZUM GUTENBERG

Little is known about the father of modern printing, and most of what we do know comes from a series of lawsuits that indicate that Gutenberg was a busy entrepreneur — but not a very successful one. He was born around 1400 to a patrician family in eastern Germany and lived his life between Mainz and Strasbourg. Gutenberg was a trained jeweler and goldsmith. The answers to how he developed an interest in books and why he turned inventor are unknown.

We do, however, know almost certainly when his inventing began in earnest: In 1448, Gutenberg received a 150-guilder loan from a cousin. Soon after, he got additional backing of 800 guilders from the merchant Johann Fust. Since a master craftsman earned about 30 guilders a year and could buy a stone house for as little as 80, Gutenberg was clearly burning through a considerable amount of seed money.

By 1450, Gutenberg had an operational press that was turning out pamphlets and flyers, but he needed a big idea — a marketing coup that would get his invention and his name out to the public. In 1452, Fust invested another 800 guilders, this time for one specific purpose: to print a new edition of the Bible.

THE HEART OF AN INNOVATION

There were a number of technologies and practices that made Gutenberg's press possible, most of which had nothing to do with Gutenberg. There was the introduction of paper, which was less expensive and far more abundant than the animal-skin vellum that most books had been made from, and there were also new inks that would stick better on paper. Then there was a demand for books among scholars and literate professionals — lawyers, doctors, generals, businesspeople — who required specialized reference works. And, since these potential customers were dispersed throughout Europe, there needed to be secure international trade routes to ensure the books could reach them safely.

Finally, there was printing itself, which was already a very old technology. The revolutionary aspect of Gutenberg's movable type printing press was not the *printing press* part but the *movable type* part.

Before Gutenberg, printed books were made by means of impressions that were carved by hand out of blocks of wood, one whole page at a time. The process was very time-consuming and no more efficient than simply copying books by hand, which was the standard method of duplication. Gutenberg's brilliant idea was to make molds for individual, reusable characters. This was difficult, exacting work, but once a complete set of molds had been made, individual characters could be mass-produced at a rate of about four per minute.

Cast in a sturdy lead alloy, Gutenberg's modular type could be used to set page after page of text. Once the type was set, a press could churn out up to 16 pages per hour, whereas a scribe was luck to copy a few pages in a whole day of labor. Europe was poised on a potential information boom.

SUCCESS... AND FAILURE

To print a Bible was a bold idea but an unlikely business decision. Since the thirteenth century, the Bible market had been sluggish. Most everyone who needed one already had one, and few could use — or afford — multiples. Deeply in debt, Gutenberg knew that the fate of his press depended on producing a best seller, the first in publishing history. Gutenberg's new edition of the Bible was priced at 20 guilders, with a deluxe vellum version selling for 50. When it was completed in 1455, the entire run of 180 copies immediately sold out.

But immediately wasn't soon enough for Gutenberg's partner, Johann Fust, who promptly took the publisher to court to collect on his loan. Fust won and took Gutenberg's press in lieu of money. To add insult to injury, he also took Gutenberg's foreman, Peter Schoeffer. Henceforth, it was Furst and Schoeffer who would be the driving force of the printing revolution and see the fledgling industry through its perilous early days.

Gutenberg tried with little success to start up a new press. He did not, however, pass into compete obscurity. In 1465, the bishop of Mainz wrote to Gutenberg, praising him for his invention and awarding him a pension — 2,000 liters of wine, 2,000 liters of grain, and a new suit of clothes every year.

Gutenberg died in 1468.

THE BOOK BUBBLE

Gutenberg did not fare so well, but his invention did. Within 40 years of the release of Gutenberg's Bible, more than 200 printers had sprung up across Europe and were turning out thousands of books each year.

The impact of the printing press on Renaissance society was very much like that of the Internet 500 years later — for better and for worse. On the one hand, much faster means of reproduction and expanded outlets spawned an incredible profusion of information. On the other hand, sheer abundance devalued writing in general. Authors were paid very little, publishers took most of the profit, and even then many publishers went bankrupt. With no copyright restrictions, an unscrupulous printer could rush a cheap knock-off of an upcoming book and saturate the market while the original was still being assembled. And unscrupulous printers were the rule rather than the exception.

Initially, intellectuals were enthusiastic about the press because they envisioned easy access to history's storehouse of ideas — much as technophiles would later tout the promise of digitized texts. However, preparing an edition for publication was a very expensive endeavor — vastly more than transcribing an individual book the traditional way. The only way for publishers to turn a profit was to sell lots of books. But to the scholars' dismay there was no mass market for rediscovered philosophy or the untranslated poetry of obscure Ancient Greeks.

Instead, what kept the presses running were inexpensive pamphlets and single-page flyers called *broadsides*. Venomous attacks on political or religious rivals, almanacs, transcripts of popular plays, or colorful accounts of parades, firework displays, and other royal pageantry — that was the stuff that buyers wanted. Then, as now, the prophecies of Nostradamus were also best sellers. And, of course, there was porn.

Most of the more idealistic first wave of book publishers did not last into the sixteenth century. But the book industry survived. By 1600, 150 years after the first movable-type-printed book, an estimated 350,000 individual titles had been printed, topping perhaps 100 million copies. ●

THE DIVINE RIGHT OF KINGS

"God gives not Kings the style of Gods in vain,
For on his Throne his Scepter do they sway:
And as their subjects ought them to obey,
So Kings should fear and serve their God again
If then ye would enjoy a happy reign,
Observe the Statutes of your heavenly King,
And from his Law, make all your Laws to spring:
Since his Lieutenant here ye should remain,
Reward the just, be steadfast, true, and plain,
Repress the proud, maintaining aye the right,
Walk always so, as ever in his sight,
Who guards the godly, plaguing the profane:
  And so ye shall in Princely virtues shine,
  Resembling right in your mighty King Divine."

— JAMES I OF ENGLAND, SONNET IN THE
OPENING OF *BASILIKON DORON*, 1599

TIME OF ORIGIN: *1598*

ORIGIN IN: *Scotland*

HYPE FACTOR: *9 — Who better to advertise and implement radical political ideas than the reigning monarch himself?*

IMPACT FACTOR: *8 — Ironically, the failed attempt to institute an absolute monarchy in England and the altogether too successful one in France fostered a democratic reaction that's proven to be much more enduring.)*

We may have images in our minds of monarchs screaming, *"Off with their heads!,"* making war on a whim, and marrying and divorcing princesses at will, but for most of the Middle Ages, kings were hardly all-powerful despots. Even in kingdoms that didn't have written constitutions (which were most of them), there were substantial constraints on monarchs: tradition and the raw facts of power. Without the backing of a full purse and loyal dukes, kingship was just an empty title.

It was only on the brink of the modern era that the venerable but seldom invoked divine right of kings was most fully articulated as a political theory and put into practice. (Spoiler alert: It didn't work out so well.)

A PHILOSOPHER KING

The idea that a monarch rules as a god incarnate or at the pleasure of a divinity is very ancient, going back at least to the Egyptian pharaohs and the temple-states of the Middle East. In medieval Europe, the rhetoric of the divine right of kings was employed from time to time, but it didn't emerge as a sustained political position until after the Reformation.

When Martin Luther challenged the authority of the pope in 1517, he unintentionally created a power vacuum. If the head of the church was no longer the supreme spiritual authority in Christendom, who was? For many Protestants, the answer was clear: each individual. But the position was not

undisputed. Some thinkers believed that, for the sake of domestic harmony, the pope's prerogative should devolve to the kings, each of whom would be free to direct the spiritual life of his own nation.

While issues of religion and politics were contested with extreme violence and cruelty in continental Europe, Great Britain was mostly spared, and it was in this comparatively tranquil setting that an obscure Scottish monarch, James VI, penned the most thoughtful justification of the divine right of kings and their freedom to rule absolutely, a treatise he called *The True Law of Free Monarchies*.

James was that rare example of a king who fancied himself an intellectual and who just might have had the brains to back it up. Nevertheless, his political philosophy might well have gone nowhere, were it not for the fact that James also happened to be a not-so-distant relative of the childless and now elderly Queen Elizabeth of England. When she died, in 1603, James VI of Scotland became James I of England, and his profile among world leaders was raised considerably.

AN ABSOLUTE MONARCH

As king of England, James I was too busy trying to stay out of the religious wars that were tearing Europe apart to put into full practice his idea of absolute monarchy, but he did find the time at least twice to revise and republish his political writings, including *Basilikon Doron*. Its title Greek for "The King's Gift," the book was written by James for his heirs, and its contents are aptly summarized by the sonnet quoted above. In James' thought, the king was God's lieutenant, with absolute freedom to act. He could make any laws he chose, but he himself was exempt from them — although a good king, of course, would make only just laws and voluntarily submit to his own injunctions… so long as it was convenient.

When Charles I assumed the throne in 1625, he had inherited his father's taste for autocracy but none of his political savvy and personal charm. The new King's high-handed style antagonized Parliament, and his tolerant attitude toward Catholicism drew suspicion from the more hard-edged Puritans. Animosity between Charles and Parliament grew until a furious Charles dismissed the consultative body and attempted to rule on his own, a true, absolute monarch.

This period of personal rule lasted 11 years. Poverty eventually forced Charles to recall Parliament because it had constitutional powers over taxation that not even the king could usurp. But the relationship was beyond repair. When Charles attempted to bring trumped-up charges of treason against five members of the House of Commons, the House responded with actual treasonous defiance. Soon, a full-blown civil war broke out.

THE LAW OF UNINTENDED CONSEQUENCES

England's first and only absolute monarch was captured, tried, and executed in 1649 for treason. Charles I's clumsy management ended his reign, ended his life, and, temporarily, ended the English monarchy. In 1660, a counterrevolution restored the throne, but only through a compromise that gave Parliament greater powers. For Britain, the era of the divine right of kings was over.

In France, the divine right of kings had a somewhat more successful run, climaxing during the splendid reign of the Sun King, Louis XIV (1638–1715). But it ended in even worse disaster for that monarchy: the French Revolution.

In both England and France, implementing the ideals of absolute monarchy generated an intellectual counterreaction that lauded the rights of individual freedom, dignity, and self-determination, the core values that would shape the Enlightenment of the eighteenth century and inspire more than a century of democratic revolutions throughout Europe and the New World. ●

MAGNETIC PHILOSOPHY

"But what is it that carries the planets around the Sun — for Tycho and Copernicus agree on this point — what then but a magnetic effluvium from the Sun? Truly, what is it that makes the planets eccentric from the Sun, that compels them to approach the Sun and to recede from it? Obviously an effluvium from the bodies of the planets themselves...."

— JOHANNES KEPLER, 1605

TIME OF ORIGIN: *1600*

ORIGIN IN: De Magnete, *by William Gilbert*

HYPE FACTOR: *8 — The implications of magnetic philosophy stimulated a generation of astronomers and added heat to the cosmological debates of the early seventeenth century.*

IMPACT FACTOR: *4 — Although its cosmological claims were incorrect, magnetic philosophy helped make Newtonian gravity imaginable.*

The sixteenth and seventeenth centuries are a fascinating period in the history of science because they were so energetic, so eclectic, and so incredibly *un*scientific. Ideas that today would seem questionable or downright nutty were then considered thoroughly mainstream, and even the most rigorously scientific minds were not immune to them. To give just one high-profile example, Sir Isaac Newton, the man who would give us physics and calculus, also practiced alchemy and fervently believed that the time of Christ's return could be mathematically calculated. And why not? Math had already predicted the motions of the heavenly bodies. Weren't the movements of God the next logical step?

Magnetic philosophy was a short-lived but influential intellectual trend pioneered by the English physician and early scientist William Gilbert. Like many ideas of its age, magnetic philosophy had one foot in empirical science and another in magic and spiritualism. But in the period before gravity and the laws of motion were fully formulated, it offered the first physical support to the controversial Copernican astronomical model, which correctly put the Sun, not the Earth, at the center of the cosmos.

STAR WARS

To assume that the Earth is the center of all creation is a most common-sense position — after all, it's consistent with two indisputable facts: (1) Things fall down, and (2) the Sun and the planets clearly move across the sky.

That is simplicity itself. But everything else about this geocentric theory, which was most fully developed by the second-century Alexandrine astronomer Ptolemy, is extraordinarily complex. To produce an Earth-centered model that corresponds with astronomical observations requires each planet to follow two orbits: one around the Earth, modified by another, smaller orbit, or *epicycle*, that revolves around… well, nothing. To keep the Sun, the Moon, and the five (then known) planets from plummeting straight into us, each was imagined to be contained within its own invisible, crystalline shell that guided the heavenly body along its orbits and provided it with the motive power to defy gravity when it rose back up again in its daily course. Or maybe that power came from a "soul" or "intelligence" that animated each planet. It wasn't quite clear. Furthermore, to say that the Ptolemaic system was Earth-centered is itself a simplification: The actual center of the universe had to be slightly above the Earth; otherwise, there wouldn't be seasons.

In short, the Ptolemaic system was a mess. But it worked — and, considering the incredibly complex mathematics that went into turning astronomical observations into a coherent model of the cosmos, that alone was quite the achievement.

Sometime in the early 1500s, though, a Polish mathematician and astronomer, Nicolaus Copernicus, ran the numbers again and devised a simpler system. While the math was as difficult as ever, Copernicus's model required fewer premises — just a fixed but revolving Sun at the center of the universe and an orbiting and rotating Earth with a slightly tilted axis. On the negative side, however, Copernicus's premises could be seen as contradicting certain passages of the Bible, and they definitely violated the laws of physics as currently understood, which raised troubling questions for which there was no answer, such as, "Why do the planets spin?" "Why don't we fall off the Earth?" and, for that matter, "What keeps the planets from spinning off to God knows where?"

Mindful of these potential theological and scientific heresies, Copernicus kept his new cosmological model on the down-low. As rumors of his audacious idea inevitably spread, though, Copernicus yielded to pressure from fellow intellectuals and, in 1543, published his theory. Despite its daring argument, *De Revolutionibus Orbium Coelestium* (*On the Revolutions of the Heavenly Orbs*) was not censored nor did its author face censure from the church — but the book did ignite a roaring intellectual debate.

WHAT'S SO BIG ABOUT MATH?

One reason that the church did not object to Copernicus's theory is that it was regarded as merely a mathematical model. There was nothing preventing anyone from using the Copernican system as a convenient predictive tool while still acknowledging that Earth was *really* the center of the universe. It was just math, nothing more.

That attitude might puzzle us denizens of the data-driven era, when numbers speak for themselves and with their own authority. But let's try moving the burden of proof: Why *should* any reasonable person believe that mathematical equations can explain the phenomena we see around us? What guarantees that strings of abstract numbers have *any* relationship with objective reality?

As early as the age of the pharaohs, humankind recognized the practical value of geometry. Applied to everything from drawing property lines to constructing temples and diverting water, it was an invaluable science. But even the Ancient Greeks, who made a fetish of bisecting angles and attempting to square the circle with nothing more than a straight edge and a compass, knew that geometry was an abstraction. The world was far too sloppy and unruly to be captured in points, lines, and angles. And so they had to invent another world, one that consisted only of ideas and existed only there as well. It was in this ideal realm where logic and math reigned and philosophers spun their theories — but in the coarse, material world, we applied them the best we could.

Why should this resistant Earth be any more submissive to algebra? And even if it were, what could be the significance of any mathematical equation? Math might *describe* the mechanics of some action — but what could it *tell* us about that action, what could it reveal about its meaning and its purpose? Nothing.

But in the slow unfolding of what's called the Scientific Revolution, natural philosophy and math were united. It's probable that Copernicus believed not just that his system worked but that it was also an accurate representation of reality. It's certainly true that his successors — Kepler, Galileo, Newton, and so many others — did. And that's why the heliocentrism-vs.-geocentrism debate became so fierce in the seventeenth century: It wasn't just numbers that were being argued anymore; it was reality.

WILLIAM GILBERT AND THE BIRTH OF EXPERIMENTAL SCIENCE

Okay, maybe that heading is a little hyped. We inquisitive humans have been experimenting since the dawn of time. How else did we learn that it's all right to eat slimy oysters but not the orange-like fruit of the strychnine tree? But empirical testing, like math, has not always been an accepted part of the scientific project. The world was simply too complex and our means of measurement too imprecise to make experimentation an especially reliable avenue to knowledge. To the Aristotelian scholastics who dominated the universities until the seventeenth century, a much more reliable approach to understanding was provided by deductive reasoning, which is bulletproof, so long as you start with valid premises. The problem was that during the Renaissance more and more long-standing premises were being questioned and found to be not especially valid.

When William Gilbert entered Cambridge University in 1558, at the age of 14, he received a typical late-medieval education. Studying for his MD, he read the canonical books of Galen, the second-century Roman physician who had continued to dominate medicine. Gilbert also was taught Aristotelian logic and physics and Ptolemaic astronomy, complete with epicycles and crystal shells and planetary intelligences.

You may have noticed, as Gilbert himself did, that all his intellectual authorities had been dead for at least 1,300 years. A lot had happened in that time — and most of it had hardly penetrated the universities. More congenial to the curious and independent-minded Gilbert was the intellectually engaged and innovative atmosphere of late-Elizabethan London. The center of a kingdom rapidly growing into a global maritime empire was a magnet for capable and practical men such as skilled civil and military engineers and veteran sailors with tales of new worlds.

Gilbert made a success of himself, eventually rising to become president of the Royal College of Physicians and personal physician to Queen Elizabeth I and to her successor, James I. But when he wasn't doctoring, Gilbert devoted himself to his hobby, magnetism. Unlike the typical academic of his time, Gilbert actually went out to consult experts: the craftsmen who worked with magnets to make compasses, and the experienced navigators who used them and had collected data from all over the world.

Stranger still, he invested in scientific apparatus, particularly *terrellae*, or "little Earths," spheres carved out of lodestone, that he used to plumb the mysteries of magnetism firsthand. Placing his *terrellae* on small wooden ships, he documented a free-floating magnet's tendency to rotate; by painstakingly moving a small compass over the surface of another magnetic sphere, he attempted to duplicate the anomalies and variations that old sea hands had related to him; by rubbing pieces of amber, he produced an attractive effect, which he called *electricitas* and which we know by its Anglicized name: electricity. (Although Gilbert was pleased to lambaste the narrow-mindedness and conservatism of his professors, he, like every other serious thinker of his era, wrote in Latin.)

DE MAGNETE

As the engine that drove the compass, the essential tool for ocean navigation, magnetism was of considerable practical interest in the era of sea exploration that followed the discovery of America, but the phenomenon was very poorly understood. Gilbert spent a purported 18 years and £5,000 (a fantastically large sum back then) to write the definitive book on the magnet — in fact, he called it *De Magnete*, or *On the Magnet* — which he published in 1600. Although Gilbert's book is hardly remembered anymore, *De Magnete* could reasonably be called the first ever work of experimental science.

In six volumes, the author summarizes previous approaches to the topic — most of which he gleefully eviscerates — before adding the reports that he himself collected and verified, and, finally, offering the results of his own experimentation and (remarkably correct) conclusions — which included his observations on the all but unheard of phenomenon of electricity.

But Gilbert had a broader vision than merely aiding navigation or explaining static cling. His chief aim in publishing was to promulgate his cosmological vision, which he called "magnetical philosophy." The Aristotelian physics he had learned in college posited two sets of physical laws: one that governed the rarified celestial realm and another for our fallen and imperfect Earth. Gilbert, on the other hand, believed that the Earth was as noble as any other planet, that it was regulated by the same principles, and that it, too, possessed a soul. Flowing forth spontaneously from the heart of Mother Earth (his expression) was her soul, the wellspring of the magnetic force. It was this power that caused the Earth to rotate, and, by Gilbert's reckoning, this argument of his was the first to demonstrate the physical evidence supporting Copernicus's model of the solar system. It was no longer just a mathematical abstraction; it reflected a physical reality.

Talk of planetary souls is well out of bounds for today's scientists, which is one reason why Gilbert is largely forgotten. But even if on the larger points Gilbert was partially or wholly incorrect, his attempt to substantiate heliocentrism with physical arguments inspired a generation of astronomers, and it's no exaggeration to say that he set them on a path that made Newton's formulation of gravity all but inevitable.

MAXIMUM MAGNET

Gilbert's book became an intellectual must-read. As an emerging technology, the magnet suggested seductive possibilities — could a modification of the compass somehow allow sailors to determine their latitude as well as their direction? Since magnets produced spin, could they be made into engines? Were there medical applications?

Galileo was among those influenced by the ideas in *De Magnete*, and so, especially, was Johannes Kepler. In the same works where he lays out his laws of planetary motion, Kepler argues from analogy to Gilbert that the Sun must be a magnet, radiating, just as it does heat and light, some other force that impels the planets along their orbits.

But for all the intellectual boost he gave to the Copernican system, Gilbert also indirectly raised the heat of the controversy. Now that the Copernican partisans — such as that infamous pain-in-the-neck Galileo — were undeniably making truth claims about reality, the Catholic hierarchy was forced to choose between science and dogma. Caught up in the reactionary zeal of the Counter-Reformation, the church sided with dogma.

In 1616, the Vatican banned Copernicus's *De Revolutionibus* and all other books advocating heliocentrism. In the wake of this ruling, at least five books were published by Jesuit intellectuals specifically attacking magnetic philosophy, which had provided intellectual support to heliocentrism. Rather than cause the Earth to rotate, these defenders of the faith argued, a magnetic core would fix the planet even more immovably in place; moreover, magnetism itself could not account for the orderly movement of the planets; and, most irrefutable of all, an Earth-size magnet, as envisioned by Gilbert, would attract all iron objects to itself with irresistible strength.

Nevertheless, the religious objection to magnetism extended only to its support for a Sun-centered universe. Father Athanasius Kircher, who launched a particularly trenchant refutation of Gilbert's and Kepler's magnetic ideas, had mastered his material so thoroughly because he was also a great enthusiast of magnetism. Something of an eccentric genius, or perhaps just a crackpot, Kircher alluded in florid language to the wondrous potential of magnets and hinted that he was engaged in breakthrough research that would revolutionize surveying... or maybe communications. In the end, however, nothing panned out.

In fact, after the initial hype, magnetism turned out to be a general disappointment. None of the projected magnetic innovations emerged — no motors, no medicines, no telecommunications devices. By 1660, the trend was over. There was no decisive repudiation, just years of unfulfilled promise. Eventually, people just lost interest and went on to the next big thing.

GRAVITY: THE NEW MAGNETISM

In 1687, Isaac Newton published his laws of motion in *Philosophiæ Naturalis Principia Mathematica* (*The Mathematical Principles of Natural Philosophy*), which was simultaneously the culmination of seventeenth-century natural philosophy and the cornerstone of a fully fledged, math-based, and empirically focused modern science.

Among Newton's achievements was his equation for gravity, which, taken with the laws of planetary motion formulated by Johannes Kepler, at last gave a comprehensive physical explanation for how a Sun-centered cosmos would work and provided devastating proof of why an Earth-centered arrangement would not.

Newton had done the math, but the idea that the cosmos is bound by an insubstantial force that varies with the mass of an object and acts instantly over distance is pure magnetic philosophy, minus the magnet. •

THE GREAT MASCULINE RENUNCIATION

"Let your dress be as cheap as may be without shabbiness."

— WILLIAM COBBETT, *ADVICE TO YOUNG MEN*, 1829

TIME OF ORIGIN: *Late seventeenth to early nineteenth centuries*

ORIGIN IN: *England*

HYPE FACTOR: *7 — All the media of the era, from novels to newspaper articles to sermons to political speeches, condemned decadent and effeminate luxury in men's clothing and praised modest and thrifty understatement.)*

IMPACT FACTOR: *7 — We still feel the effects today, from the business suit to the enduring conventional wisdom that men's fashion should be classic and timeless.*

If, as a man, your morning grooming ritual does not include re-powdering the shoulder-length curls of your wig, smoothing the wrinkles from your lace-covered blouse, brushing out the nap of your velvet doublet, and lacing the silk ribbons of your high-heeled shoes, you may thank (or blame, according to your taste) a power struggle between British aristocrats and a growing middle class that incidentally redefined the look of masculinity at the dawn of the modern era.

Dubbed "the great masculine renunciation" by a fashion historian in the 1930s, this was the moment when men and women's fashion decisively parted ways. Bright colors and lacy ruffles did not suit the new masculine virtues of hard work, thrift, and sober judgment. Henceforth, somber colors and austere cuts would characterize male dress. With only brief and occasional periods of fanciful sartorial rebellion, it's a dress code that endures today.

"FOR THE APPAREL OFT PROCLAIMS THE MAN"

While we today tend to think that the way a person dresses is a matter of personal taste, historically clothes have been an important means of showing status. Famously, purple dye was the marker of Rome's senatorial class, and when rising wealth put this expensive extract from a rare species of Mediterranean sea snail within the reach of prosperous middle class, the restriction was written into law. By a later decree, no one but the emperor was allowed to wear red shoes.

The cultural assumption that a person's social status should be directly reflected in his clothing budget is laid out by Shakespeare in advice Polonius gives his son Laertes in Act 3 of *Hamlet*:

> Costly thy habit as thy purse can buy,
> But not expressed in fancy; rich, not gaudy,
> For the apparel oft proclaims the man.

According to the Bard, with regard to human society, you *should* be able to judge the book by its cover: Courtiers should look like courtiers, and peasants like peasants. Class was the major distinction, so, at the highest level of Renaissance society, men and women alike wore the most luxurious and flashiest outfits. Silk, velvet, and fur; floral embroidery; gold threads; pearl and gem adornments — all were equally available to the sexes. It was even men who adopted high heels first (it was an exaggerated cavalry fashion — high heels helped keep stirrups in place) and who flashed their shapely legs in tight silk hose, while women were more modestly covered from neck to ankle.

"A NATION OF SHOPKEEPERS"

In the eighteenth century, England became the center of a prospering mercantilist empire. As a flood of new wealth raised people out of lower stations in life, a new social figure emerged: the gentleman — a person of common birth but gentle instinct, well-mannered, sound of judgment, pragmatic, modest, full of common sense: He united free-market virtues with aristocratic courtesy and refinement.

It was this marked interest in commerce and the thrifty values that go with it that led Napoléon to quip that "England is a nation of shopkeepers."

As every level of society responded to the changes of new wealth, new values, and new members infiltrating the middle class, Enlightenment England became much preoccupied with matters of good judgment and correct behavior. The age produced three major philosophical works on aesthetics (by David Hume, Edmund Burke, and Bishop Berkeley, respectively, if you're interested); in popular culture, journalists Joseph Addison and Sir Richard Steele, writing for the *Spectator*, took the message of manners and discernment to the streets and the coffeehouses, while, in private parlors, the new reading craze, the novel, offered endless object lessons in behaviors to be emulated or shunned.

But the focus on congenial surfaces concealed a profound trauma. Just as the neurotic drive for normality in 1950s America was a reaction to the uncertainty of the Depression and the horrors of the Second World War, Georgian England's fetishizing of manners was a reaction to a vicious civil war. In 1641, long-standing tensions — between Parliament and Crown, between the English and the Scots, between those who hated Catholics a little and those who hated them a lot — precipitated a period of violence that culminated in the imprisonment and execution of King Charles I. [See **The Divine Right of Kings**]

The civil war and the tumultuous half century that followed it left the nation deeply shaken. When a reconciled king and Parliament declared a United Kingdom of Great Britain in 1707, all sides were given a chance to start over and forget old differences in the new, unifying idea of Britishness. It is no accident that the hallmarks of the Briton even to this day are good manners and repression.

Even as middle-class gentlemen were learning to flex their political power and look respectable doing so, the elite recognized that it was time for them to clean up their act or lose their legitimacy. Charles II — the so-called Merry Monarch — may have flaunted the dozen illegitimate children he'd had with no fewer than half a dozen mistresses, but in this new sober age of commerce, such displays of lovable roguishness were simply not good for business.

So both sides of the political spectrum — the gentry, who saw themselves as guarding traditional institutions against an onslaught from the grubby bean-counters, and the virtuous bourgeoisie, who sought to purge the nation of the poison spread by a decadent, luxurious, and useless aristocracy — could agree on one point: Masculinity was properly expressed through self-denial, sobriety, and thrift. It was all right for ladies to care about clothes and jewelry — they were flighty by nature and well suited to such trivialities. But political power depended on sound judgment, and the man of judgment was deaf to the whimsical call of fashion.

Conspicuous display now signified aristocratic decadence, nouveau riche insecurity, or an unseemly social climbing. True power didn't care about vain display and could afford to conceal itself. This antifashion stance of course became its own fashion, which triggered an escalating competition of "inconspicuous consumption," with each side vying to appear the most earnest and unobtrusive.

Revolutionary War-era men's fashion might look ostentatious to us today, but French visitors to England frequently remarked on the plainness and uniformity of British menswear. By the early nineteenth century, British men's clothing had become almost in fact a uniform: navy or brown coat, vest, white breeches, and black boots. As democratic ideals spread throughout Europe, so too did this more sober style, which today can be recognized as the ancestor of the business suit. •

SCIENTIFIC RACISM

"In disposition the negro is joyous, flexible, and indolent; while the many nations which compose this race present a singular diversity of intellectual character, of which the far extreme is the lowest grade of humanity."

— SAMUEL MORTON, FROM *CRANIA AMERICANA*

TIME OF ORIGIN: *1839*

ORIGIN IN: Crania Americana, *by Samuel Morton*

HYPE FACTOR: *6 — Hardly anyone could afford to buy* Crania Americana, *and the details of its findings were confined mostly to the scientific community.*

IMPACT FACTOR: *8 — The gist of its argument, however, was used broadly to give a gloss of scientific support to flat-out racism during the lead-up to the Civil War.*

It's no hyperbole to maintain, as many do, that racism is America's original sin. But when people say that, it's generally slavery and the still-lingering ramifications of that particularly cruel and wicked institution that they have in mind and not *racism* itself — after all, human beings have been demonizing each other over racial differences since the beginning of time, right?

Well, yes, and no. *Race* as we understand it today is a relatively new idea that hardly predates our nation. And, in fact, it was early ethnologists, physiologists, and anthropologists here in America who did much of the seminal work in race science that still reverberates today. As you might suspect, some of them had an explicit agenda of racial inequality that they were attempting to verify. But many of them didn't — and that's almost more troubling.

A HEADHUNTER IN PHILADELPHIA

One of the more vile threads in the historic weft of science begins with a stooped and somewhat sickly man, whose geniality in person was equaled only by his scrupulousness and detachment in the laboratory.

Though all but forgotten today, Samuel George Morton was a scientific superstar in the early days of the republic. He earned his MD at the University of Pennsylvania in 1820 and then earned a *second* one at the University of Edinburgh, which, though in decline, was still one of the most prestigious medical schools in the English-speaking world.

Morton's early research on fossils collected by the Lewis and Clark Expedition earned him the decidedly unpoetic honorific *the Father of American Invertebrate Paleontology*, and he would have the further distinction of being among the nation's first physical anthropologists. A member of the prestigious American Philosophical Society, Morton was secretary and, later, president of the Academy of Natural Sciences, the nation's first natural science research institution. At the time of his death in 1851, this lifelong Philadelphian was lauded in a newspaper obituary as America's most well known scholar.

In 1830, however, Morton's career took a decisive — and infamous — turn, when he lost his head to the up-and-coming scientific vogue for skull collecting.

According to Morton's own account, the fastidious professor was preparing visual aids for a lecture on the hot new theory out of Germany about the Five Races of Man, when he came up two skulls short. Caucasian and Negro skulls were a breeze to procure, and just a little legwork turned up a couple of Indian heads. But much to Morton's dismay, not a single skull of a Mongolian or Malay could by any means be acquired anywhere in Philadelphia, which was then the nation's intellectual capital.

Chagrined by this poor showing of American science, Morton resolved to singlehandedly address the skull shortage by starting his own collection. Calling upon his considerable social and professional network, Morton was able to obtain within a single year some 100 heads, for cash or favors. This might sound bizarre today, but throughout the nineteenth century there was a booming (and only *slightly* illegal) trade in medical cadavers. Burial grounds, battlefields, and hospital morgues alike were plundered

RACE AS A CONSTRUCTION

To say that race is a construction — that is to say, a concept with a history — and not a natural, unchanging given is not to deny that groups of people broadly share physical similarities. What it does assert, however, is that the similarities that are perceived as meaningful — and the specific meanings ascribed to them — change over time.

According to the way we've been conditioned, for example, having pale skin, exceptional height, and a preference for beer over wine is understood to reveal something fundamental about a person, while, on the other hand, having large ears, an outie bellybutton, and a taste for dark rather than white turkey meat says nothing at all.

The fact that racial borders correspond with geographical divisions should be a big clue that race has historically been used — intentionally or not — as a means of redefining arbitrary cultural differences as immutable biological ones. In the eyes of the nineteenth-century racial theorist, Europe was destined to rule the globe, not because of a complex web of history, culture, and natural resources that gave the West a vast technological advantage, but because of an inherent racial superiority.

by enterprising and daring "resurrectionists," who kept anatomists and doctors-in-training supplied with a steady stream of research specimens. By 1849, Morton put his personal count at 867 human skulls and another 601 from "inferior animals."

THE HUMAN ANIMAL

In the mid-nineteenth century, the life sciences were still very much in the "collect and name" stage. While astronomy, physics, and chemistry had entered the Enlightenment as genuine speculative sciences, biology historically had lagged until the great era of sea exploration. Beginning around the late seventeenth century, naturalists scrambled to catalogue the bonanza of unfamiliar life forms that were flowing back to Europe from distant lands.

Down through the mid-nineteenth century, biologists were still primarily natural historians, who regarded their job as classifying rather than theorizing and experimenting. Their collective goal was to compile the universal book of life, wherein every species, unvarying and uniquely crafted by the hand of God himself, was defined and assigned to its proper link in the great chain of being that led from the most primitive molds up through plants and increasingly complex animals, all the way up to the Creator's noblest achievement: humankind.

The most influential of the early classifiers, or *taxonomists*, was the Swedish zoologist Carl Linnaeus, who invented the convention of binomial nomenclature that we all remember from school (e.g., you and I are *Homo sapiens*, while my cat is *Felis catus*, and the flea that is currently molesting him is *Ctenocephalides felis*).

In the 1767 edition of Linnaeus' foundational and much-revised work *Systema Naturae* (*The System of Nature*), Linnaeus brought human beings into the great web of nature by introducing his five divisions of humankind: *Americanus*, *Asiaticus*, *Africanus*, *Europeanus*, and *Monstrosus*. (Despite appearances, that last category doesn't actually mean *monstrous*. It's more like *miscellaneous*, covering varieties of human attested to in mythology but not yet substantiated.)

Beyond labeling them, Linnaeus had little to say about the races. That task was taken up by the German scholar Johan Friedrich Blummenbach, who, around 1775, discarded Linnaeus's Monster class and divided the Asian into two varieties: northern Mongols and southern Malays.

Blummenbach's classifications were based on careful measurements he made of sample skulls, with particular attention being given to the inline of the forehead. It was Blummenbach's classification system and techniques of *craniometry* — or *skull measurement* — that Samuel Morton had intended to explicate in his fateful lesson from 1830.

QUANTIFIABLE SUPERIORITY

In the intervening decades, the scientific consensus was shifting about the varieties of human being. Enlightenment thinkers such as Blummenbach and Linnaeus were largely in agreement that there was but a single species of human, which had descended from Adam and Eve and diversified as it spread throughout the world, each tribe adapting slightly to suit its environment. While it was assumed that the Caucasian, or White, race was

RACE BEFORE THERE WAS RACE

In Classical antiquity, the set of meaningful human differences was very different from today's. For the Greeks, feelings of "racial" belonging were expressed at a very local level. Athenian, Spartan, Corinthian, Theban — it was your citizenship that indicated whether you were probably warlike or bookish, whether — if poetry was your bag — you were more naturally suited to be a tragedian, epigrammist, or comedian. But while neighboring city-states might occasionally be deadly rivals, the citizens, as fellow Greek speakers, were also united in their disdain for uncultured foreigners, *barbaroi* — barbarians — who got this name because they ba-ba-babbled like animals (which shows that people don't have to resort to full-fledged racism to find ways of being chauvinist jerks).

The Romans were more cosmopolitan. Of course, they had their stereotypes: Greeks were dishonest; Germans were savage but honorable; Egyptians were brainy. But what mattered above all was Roman-ness — and that could be learned. If you spoke good Latin and did Roman things like worshiping the Emperor and going to the baths daily, you were in. It didn't matter if you were black or brown or white.

Of course, Classical philosophers pondered the obvious physical and temperamental differences among peoples. Their consensus was that large-scale human variation was primarily an accident of geography. A straightforward example was the dark skin of the Nubians, which was caused by the hot African sun. It was a more mysterious climactic influence, however, that enervated the Persians to the east, making them less suited to the rigors of warfare but masters of political manipulation instead. The barbarians to the west were on the other extreme: While exceptional warriors, they had no sense of civic life. Occupying the ethico-climatological Goldilocks' zone, the Greco-Romans (in their own accounting) were just right: both adept soldiers and skillful politicians.

the highest in terms of innate intellect and beauty, Enlightenment ideology proposed that all human beings were born as blank slates, each equally amenable to reason and no less capable of attaining greatness.

As Europeans took a more assertive role throughout the globe, however, that free and easy egalitarianism was countered by a harsher theory. Technological and economic advantages became elided in the minds of European naturalists with cultural and, ultimately, racial superiority. It seemed self-evident that there was a natural hierarchy of races, which historical events were demonstrating but which science had not yet quantified.

For the remaining two decades of his life, Samuel Morton devoted the bulk of his attention and his meager income to providing that missing data set. Starting from the widely accepted premise that a larger brain equals greater intelligence, Morton painstakingly measured the dimensions and the cranial capacity of the hundreds of skulls in his collection. His conclusion: Europeans indeed possessed the largest skulls and therefore most advanced brains.

I'M NOT A RACIST, *BUT*...

Morton's research advanced *polygenism*, the theory that the races of humankind were so different from each other that they were actually distinct species. This was quite a radical idea at the time because it contradicted the biblical story of creation, which was almost universally accepted as historical fact. Indeed, Morton, a man who was conventional in habits and did not court controversy, avoided the term *polygenism* because he did not want to offend religious sensibilities. Nevertheless, he also tended to see himself as a scientific gadfly, like Galileo: The fact that Morton's research led him toward such an unpopular position was a sort of guarantee among his supporters of his unimpeachable dedication to the scientific method.

The fact that Morton was mildly abolitionist also immunized him from accusations of skewing his research. Like many citizens of the early republic, Morton viscerally disliked like African Americans, but he loathed slavery. Unlike Southern intellectuals who, as the drive for abolition gained momentum, were deliberately seeking justifications for one race to enslave another, Morton's political views were at odds with his scientific conclusions — and that contradiction gave his work even more authority: Morton discerned an unbridgeable and immutable inequality among the races not *because of* but *despite* his social views.

CRANIA AMERICANA

In 1839, Morton went public with his research when he self-published a lavish monograph on the skulls of Native Americans. *Crania Americana* is a monumental work in every sense. A full-sized folio work, it contained 71 nearly life-size lithographs of beautifully rendered skulls with a complete discussion of Morton's craniometric method and conclusions, plus essays on the history of the peoples of the Americas and a supplement on phrenology, a very distant intellectual forerunner of neurology, which posited that the shape of the skull indicated specific qualities of the brain within, such as intelligence, trustworthiness, and industriousness.

Unfortunately for Morton, his magnum opus was a bit too magnum for the moment: *Crania Americana* sold for $20 (about $500 in today's money), but in 1837, the US had entered a deep economic recession. Although Morton nearly bankrupted himself to pay for printing, he sold very few books.

Nevertheless, Morton's ideas circulated. While he could scarcely afford the gesture, he gave away many copies of his work to eminent colleagues. One of the most influential was the Swiss-born naturalist Louis Agassiz, who was a major force in Harvard University's zoology department and, therefore, in American science in general. An outspoken polygenist who would become a fierce opponent of Darwinism, Agassiz was also unabashedly racist — although he maintained that his personal views in no way influenced his scientific outlook — and kept Morton's ideas alive and academically respectable into the post-Civil War era.

At the mass level, Morton's ideas were spread by public lectures, which were a popular form of entertainment at the time. The self-styled Egyptologist and best-selling author George Gliddon was a particularly indefatigable Morton supporter. Part-huckster, part-intellectual, Gliddon mesmerized audiences of the P.T. Barnum era with his exhibitions of ancient mummies that he had obtained in Egypt where he had worked as a businessman and low-level diplomat. Criticized as pompous and effete by one critic, Gliddon may have been a lazy civil servant, but he demonstrated great energy and resourcefulness in his self-interest, raiding tombs and combing bazaars in the company of a shady companion he referred to in letters as simply "a snake hunter."

A business associate of Morton, Gliddon netted him 100 African skulls — sufficient fodder for Morton's second skull-book, *Crania Ægyptiaca*. Less expensive, far less lavishly illustrated, and much more overt in its racism than *Crania Americana*, Morton's new book furthered the argument for polygenism and even offered a defense of slavery — at least in the ancient world. It also sold well, thanks in large part to Gliddon's warm endorsement and his willingness to emphasize the racist implications that the author himself shied away from.

When Morton died, seven years after the publication of *Crania Ægyptiaca,* northern newspapers remembered him as versatile scientist who had studied humans, animals, and geology. The *Charleston Medial Journal,* however, preferred to eulogize him as a race-warrior: "We can only say that we of the South should consider him as our benefactor, for aiding most materially in giving the negro his true position as an inferior race."

THE LONG SHADOW

Morton's craniometric theories and techniques did not long outlive him. Polygenism eventually was toppled in the debates over evolution, while the fever for skull hunting was replaced by a movement toward brain collecting. Near the turn of the century, race theorists flocked to sociology, infamously developing ideas of social Darwinism and eugenics which had dire consequences in the twentieth century.

When Morton is remembered today, it is not as the brave truth-teller that he imagined himself to be — flouting both religious and abolitionist pieties in the name of objective science — but as a cautionary tale: Morton's studied neutrality and scrupulous avoidance of political embroilment could not exempt him from his moral responsibility. Science may exist in a moral vacuum, but ideas (wrong as well as a right) live in history and have consequences, even if we'd rather not acknowledge them. ●

THE KODAK CAMERA

"You press the button, we do the rest."

— **KODAK MOTTO**

TIME OF ORIGIN: *1888*

ORIGIN IN: *Rochester, New York*

HYPE FACTOR: *7 — Kodak's first camera wasn't especially hyped, but the company's high-profile celebration of photography lasted for an entire century.*

IMPACT FACTOR: *7 — Photography might not have eased any of the material burdens of human life, but can you imagine a world where it is all but impossible to preserve images of absent friends, loved ones, or even our departed youth?*

When, in 2014, the word *selfie* was granted entry into both *Merriam-Webster* and the Scrabble dictionary, it was taken by many as an official recognition of something they'd long realized: It's too damned easy to take pictures nowadays.

Not too long ago, photo albums were treasured family heirlooms that offered a rare tangible link to the past. Now we are awash with digital images. With one-click convenience, the data flows from our phone directly to a Facebook or Instagram page, where we may not even bother to view it again, but where it sits with an ever-growing hodgepodge of personal ephemera, trivial and profound: brunches long since devoured, shoes we never purchased, a celebrity sighting on Tenth and Broadway, wedding pictures, grainy video of a concert, images from a parent's funeral....

This urge to document our lives in such compulsive detail is not inborn. It was George Eastman, founder of the Kodak company and popularizer of amateur photography, who perhaps more than anyone else taught us to view our own past with nostalgia, to see an imperative to record it as a souvenir of our own lives and pass it down as a keepsake for our descendants. And he did it so he could sell us film.

THE FIRST PORTABLE CAMERA

The precursor to your photo app was a wood and leather box, about three inches square and six inches deep. It had a fixed lens and no viewfinder: You aimed it much as you would a rifle: by aligning two V-shaped lines inscribed on the top. And it was also, incidentally, marksmanship that gave the name to what you did with this contraption: You took snapshots.

Retailing in 1888 for $25 — which, converted to today's dollars, would make it roughly as expensive as a good desktop PC — the original Kodak camera was not cheap. But it was considerably less expensive than a professional camera.

More important, however, was the fact that it took absolutely no skill to operate: You pointed and clicked. The camera came preloaded with 100 exposures. When they were taken, you returned the camera to Kodak, and for $10 they would process and print the film and return the device, reloaded and ready for use. That was a revolutionary technical advancement.

THE ORIGINAL DISRUPTIVE COMPANY

Kodak founder George Eastman started out as an amateur photographer — although that term may be misleading. Being a camera enthusiast in the mid-1800s was like being a computer enthusiast in the 1970s: It entailed considerable technical knowledge and a high capacity for tinkering. Photographers didn't just need to understand exposure times and focal depths. They also had to process their own negatives, make their own prints, and even make their own photoplates to capture their exposures.

The state of the art at the time was the so-called wet-process plate. The manufacturing technique was a labor-intensive process that produced just single-exposure glass plates that were fragile and had to be used quickly before they dried out.

Eastman's particular bent led him toward experimenting with a dry-process alternative that could render paper photosensitive. Lengths of

THE BROWNIE

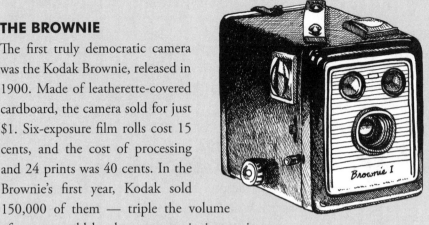

The first truly democratic camera was the Kodak Brownie, released in 1900. Made of leatherette-covered cardboard, the camera sold for just $1. Six-exposure film rolls cost 15 cents, and the cost of processing and 24 prints was 40 cents. In the Brownie's first year, Kodak sold 150,000 of them — triple the volume of cameras sold by the company in its previous record year. Initially marketed toward children, the Brownie was named after elf-like cartoon characters invented by Palmer Cox, a massively popular illustrator of the time, but the camera proved so popular that the kiddie angle was quickly dropped. The Brownie stayed in production for 70 years and went through 125 models.

this treated paper could be rolled to give multiple exposures — no more reloading between every shot — and they could be stored indefinitely. As Eastman worked out the bugs of his invention, he replaced the paper with transparent cellulose, otherwise known by a name we all recognize, even if few of us use it anymore: *film*.

Replacing an exclusive, expensive technology that demands a high level of skill with a less expensive, lower-quality product with mass appeal is called *market disruption*, to use the dearest buzzword of Silicon Valley's techno-entrepreneurs. But George Eastman got there more than a century before them. His goal had been to take photography out of the hands of professionals and put it within reach of ordinary people by making the camera "as convenient as a pencil," and his easy-to-use photographic film made that goal a real possibility. Eastman was on the verge of revolutionizing the entire photography industry — except there was no photography industry yet. So he made one.

A CLEVER WAY OF SELLING FILM

Eastman was an artful inventor, but he was a genuine genius when it came to marketing. The first thing he did after perfecting the dry process was create a brand: Kodak. He chose an intentionally meaningless combination of letters so that his trademark would be fresh, with absolutely no preexisting connotations: All it would signify was the company Eastman was creating. Next he created his killer app: An affordable, foolproof camera. Since his ultimate goal was to sell film, Eastman wanted the cheapest, no-frills camera conceivable, but it also had to be utterly reliable. To get there, he pushed the limits of mass production. Henry Ford gets the credit for employing interchangeable parts on his assembly line, but Eastman did it before him: Any part of the Kodak camera could be replaced — any screw fit any hole, and any lens and any film cartridge fit any box. It is a quality we take for granted today, but it was a milestone in efficiency.

The Kodak camera was released in May of 1888 and immediately captured some high-profile users. President Grover Cleveland bought one, as did the Dalai Lama. Gilbert and Sullivan even name-checked the invention in their light opera *Utopia* — which was sort of the nineteenth-century version of being put into a *South Park* episode. In the first six months, some 5,000 cameras flew off the shelves. Within ten years, an estimated 1.5 million had been sold.

MARKETING NOSTALGIA

Kodak quickly became synonymous with photography: Snapshots were called *Kodaks* and shutterbugs were referred to as *Kodakers*. And soon enough, a tantalizing dark side of the photography craze emerged: Newspapers and a burgeoning field of new photographic magazines, like *Photographic Times* and *Photographic Topics*, began warning the public of "camera fiends" who stalked the beaches to snap unauthorized photos of scantily clad bathers. In the UK a minor scandal erupted over the appropriateness of publishing candid pics of the royal family.

It was all marvelous publicity.

Eastman himself, though, preferred a more family-friendly marketing strategy. He knew the novelty of his camera might soon wear out, so he worked to associate amateur photography with more enduring aspects of

American culture — family life and, in particular, children. Slogans such as "Kodak as you go!" and "The snapshots you'll want tomorrow, you must take today" portrayed the camera as an ever-ready companion waiting to record the fleeting markers of ordinary life — birthdays, holidays, and family gatherings.

Eastman also recognized that, socialized to the eye of the camera, the young subjects of today would grow into the photographers of tomorrow. In 1929, Kodak sponsored its first of many amateur photography contests. Children as subjects were heavily represented, and the $250,000 grand prize went to a portrait of a toddler.

DEATH FROM AN EXCESS OF SUCCESS

The Kodak business model of bolstering photography in order sell film worked extraordinarily well for 100 years, as the company captured 80 percent of the market for photographic chemicals and paper. The one market condition it couldn't respond to, however, was the eventual obsolescence of film itself.

The deathblow came with the rise of smartphones. Where once Kodak thrived on proliferating cheap cameras and making it up on film, companies like Apple and Android were now using free camera apps as a way of selling phones — no film necessary. In 2012, after years of dwindling significance, Kodak filed for bankruptcy.

The demands of poetic justice had been met: One giant of disruptive technology was undone by the rise of a new breed of disruptive upstarts. •

FREUDIANISM

"I am not what I am."

— IAGO IN SHAKESPEARE'S *OTHELLO*, 1603

TIME OF ORIGIN: *1895*

ORIGIN IN: *Vienna, Austria*

HYPE FACTOR: *9 — Its focus on irrationality and sexuality made psychoanalysis both shocking and irresistibly fascinating.*

IMPACT FACTOR: *6 — While its results have been mixed as a therapy, the concepts of Freudian psychoanalysis continue to shape our everyday ideas about the way the mind works.*

Ever partake in a little sibling rivalry? Relieved that you're finally free of your narcissistic ex? Are your anal roommate's diatribes about kitchen cleanliness making you neurotic?

These are just a few ways that the theories of Sigmund Freud still shape the way we understand our relationships with our fellow psyche-containing human beings.

Freud didn't invent psychology. But the concepts he pioneered while establishing his subsection of the field — psychoanalysis — affected the entire study. Whether by modifying them, adopting them wholesale, or vehemently rejecting them, every field of psychology has been forced to take account of Freud's ideas.

AN ACCIDENTAL CALLING

Psychology was not Sigmund Freud's original career path. When he graduated from the University of Vienna in 1881, Freud had already shown himself to be a brilliant neurologist. But there was no money in medical research, so he reluctantly followed his professors' advice and went into practice instead. Fatefully, however, he did not give up on the brain entirely. Freud became interested in psychology, particularly hysteria, a condition in which patients present physical symptoms without actually having the underlying disease.

In 1885, Freud secured a fellowship to study in Paris under Jean-Martin Charcot, a neurologist who was famously using hypnotic suggestion to treat hysteria. Unlike most doctors of the time, Charcot believed that the disorder — whose name derives from the Greek word for *uterus* — could affect men as well as women, a position that squared with Freud's experience.

When he returned to Vienna, Freud adopted hypnotherapy, but he tried a new tack: Instead of implanting suggestions, as Charcot did, he simply encouraged his patients to talk. It was Freud's hypothesis that the root of hysteria was an unprocessed psychological trauma. If patients were encouraged to talk freely, they would eventually reveal the source of the trauma, and in exposing it they would be cured in a climactic moment of catharsis — exorcised, in a sense, of the demons that had haunted them.

THE THINKING ORGAN

Not that Freud would have conceived it quite in that way. It is easy to forget today how radically materialistic Freud's initial view of the mind was. He was part of the first generation of scientists to have grown up after Darwin. His teachers were battle-scarred veterans of the culture wars, champions of evolution when it was a far-from-popular idea. Some, like Ernst Brücke, showed a scientistic partisanship that might even be considered strict today, impatiently and imperiously waving aside ignorant superstitions like *god* or the *soul*. If an idea couldn't be expressed through the language of physics or chemistry, then it didn't count.

By the early 1800s, physicians, as a point of theory, had accepted the idea that the brain was the organ of consciousness. [See **Scientific Racism**] A more spectacular blow for materialism, though, was struck in 1828, when the chemist Friedrich Wöhler synthesized an organic compound, urea, from inorganic components — something many scientists had considered impossible. This dealt a major blow to vitalism, the accepted theory that the presence of a mysterious life force made living and nonliving matter fundamentally different. Wöhler had shown that all chemicals are simply chemicals.

The age-old dichotomy between mind and body, spirit and flesh, seemed to be resolved: It was matter all the way down. To physiologists, the brain produced thought just as the liver produced bile. One day, when all the facts were in, we'd understand how it worked. It was just a matter of time. This was the background that Freud the neurologist was coming from. Increasingly, though, he looked to the contents of the mind to heal the illnesses of the mind.

THE TALKING CURE

In 1895, Feud published *Studies in Hysteria*, which he had cowritten with Josef Breuer, an established physician and mentor who had given Freud the idea of catharsis.

Studies in Hysteria is a landmark text because it introduced the first outline for psychoanalysis, a technique for treating psychological conditions that Freud would spend the rest of his life refining. The method starts with *free association*, where the patient — or analysand — is encouraged to speak freely and candidly to the analyst. Eventually, this leads to *transference*, when the analysand projects buried feelings onto the analyst, who then reenacts through language a deeply *repressed trauma*, a psychic injury too terrible for the patient to contemplate directly but too raw to simply go away, either. Denied direct conscious attention, the trauma expresses itself indirectly, though symptoms of physical illness. By making the analysand consciously aware of the repressed trauma and guiding the patient to find a healthier resolution, the analyst will have successfully alleviated the mental illness.

Freud and Breuer had presented a bold proposition. Many physicians believed that hysteria was incurable, and no one had ever proposed such a detailed explanation of the cause of mental illness. *Studies in Hysteria* generated considerable interest. And then Freud pushed too far.

For Freud, there was one more essential element to his model: sex. Looking for a single cause that would make hysteria a well-defined disease, Freud contended that *all* hysteria was the result of sexual abuse. In Victorian Vienna, this did not go over very well. Even his mentor Breuer protested that Freud's position was too extreme — and he must have been right, too, because Freud angrily broke off what had been not just a fruitful collaboration but a deep friendship. That's a classic Freudian defense mechanism in action.

Freud eventually moderated his position but never reconciled with Breuer.

THERE ARE NO ACCIDENTS

In Freud's model of the mind, consciousness is just a small and fiercely contested patch of psychic territory. Roiling below the threshold of awareness are simmering resentments, debilitating fears, and basic drives — hunger, aggression, and sexual desire. Like malware of the mind, our subconscious subprocesses may give no clue to their existence, except for that vaguely sluggish feeling that our resources are being tapped, and then — *wham!* — panic attacks, phobias, hysterical blindness or paralysis, the psychological equivalent of a hacked checking account or an inbox overflowing with spam e-mails for fake Russian Viagra.

But it's not just in the form of spectacular dysfunction that the subconscious expresses itself. It can also sneak though in dreams, whose bizarre images, Freud contended, present a scrambled vision of secret fears and desires; or in misstatements — like when you call a teacher *Mom* or sigh, *Oh, Stan!* when you're passionately engaged with *Steve.* These "Freudian slips" (which Freud himself called *parapraxes*) are not accidental at all. Like pressurized water, subconscious impulses will find even the smallest crack to seep through.

TURNING THE FROWN UPSIDE DOWN

With its emphasis on sex and aggression, psychoanalysis was for decades resisted in Europe as an affront to tradition, good taste, and civilization itself. Perhaps it's not surprising, then, that it received a warmer reception in the US.

Our prurient fascination with sex, no less powerful then than today, gave Freudian psychoanalysis a dangerously naughty appeal. But even more important to the acceptance of Freud's theories on these shores was our national weakness for self-improvement schemes. From mesmerism to phrenology, homeopathy to Christian Science, mind healing to the power of positive thinking, Americans have historically flocked to any theory offering an avenue to greater happiness, success, and self-mastery.

Strictly speaking, though, psychoanalysis offers none of that. The Freudian view of life is very dark, full of sexual abuse, murderous revenge fantasies, and terror in the face of the innumerable forces that threaten at any moment to kill or wound us and over which we have precious little control. In this worldview, happiness is worse than a dangerous delusion. Our twin impulses to seek happiness and avoid pain — desire and denial, in other words — are the fuel that drives the perverse machine that manufactures most of our neuroses in the first place.

Nevertheless, translated through the lexicon of our national optimism, the message of psychoanalysis was: *You can become mentally healthy just by talking exclusively about yourself for an hour every week.* That was enough to start a vogue.

In 1911, a Freudian institute of psychoanalysis opened in New York. It was the first in the world outside Vienna.

Initially, psychoanalysis was popular with a small, forward-thinking, and very rich set. But successes treating soldiers with post-traumatic shock disorder from World War I and, especially, World War II and the Korean War brought analysis into the mainstream. Between 1940 and 1960, the American Psychoanalytic Association grew five times over.

REPRESSING FREUD

Starting in the mid-1960s, psychoanalysis came under increasing attack in the US. True to the anarchic spirit of the decade, the so-called anti-psychiatry movement dismissed the very concept of mental illness as an authoritarian ploy to redefine dissent as disease. Believing that there could be no objective definition of "normal," its proponents argued that psychoanalysis was a kind of "reprogramming" aimed at eradicating thought crime.

A bigger blow, however, came later with the widespread adoption of psychotherapeutic medications, particularly SSRIs, like Prozac. [See **Prozac**] Cheaper and faster-working than psychoanalysis, they were popular with patients, and even more popular with the insurance companies that were increasingly paying for mental health services.

By 1997, fewer than one million Americans were undergoing Freudian analysis. That was fewer than the number of prescriptions that were being written for Prozac every month.

A century after Freud's breakthrough insights about the mind, psychology was turning back to the brain. ●

PLASTICS

"I just want to say one word to you.... Are you listening? Plastics."

— MR. MCGUIRE IN *THE GRADUATE*, 1967

TIME OF ORIGIN: *1907*

ORIGIN IN: *Yonkers, New York*

HYPE FACTOR: *10 — There was a time when it seemed that the entire future would be made of plastic, and we were eager for it.*

IMPACT FACTOR: *9 — Our world today may not be entirely made of it, but plastic really is everywhere.*

The quote included above, from the 1967 film *The Graduate*, is one of the most famous lines in the history of cinema. It's spoken in a tone at once unctuously conspiratorial and fatuously authoritative by a family friend to Ben, a bemused college grad who's unimpressed by the life that's been scripted for him but uncertain what he can do to change it.

The joke here is not that the advice is wrong but that it's so incredibly on the nose. Since their introduction to a mass market in the 1920s, plastics had been eagerly adopted by a public learning the joys of consumerism. Easy to mold and inexpensive to manufacture, they set a standard of convenience for both consumers and producers.

But by the 1960s, the Plastic Age had acquired an edge of irony. Something that could be made into anything lacked an essential core. In the eyes of the counterculture, plastic had become a mirror for the inner lives of a generation that aspired to nothing more than a veneer of prosperity and tranquility.

It takes a special kind of material to not only define an era but also symbolize an entire way of life. So how did plastic achieve this level of infamy?

FROM COTTON BALLS TO BILLIARD BALLS

Unlikely as it may seem, the Plastic Age arose out of an ecological crisis. The moment came in 1863, when billiard ball manufacturers in New York realized that the demand for ivory was threatening to drive the elephant to extinction. Each year, some one million tons of ivory were being processed into piano keys, chess pieces, jewelry, buttons, combs, and, particularly, billiard balls. Since a single tusk could yield just eight balls, there was serious concern for the future — not so much of the elephant, perhaps, but of the popular parlor game. A $10,000 bounty was offered to anyone who could produce an acceptable imitation.

Six years later, an amateur inventor named John Wesley Hyatt came forward with celluloid. A chemically manipulated form of cotton cellulose, this rubbery substance could be molded into any shape and then hardened through heating until it was as tough as an elephant's tusk. Hyatt had invented the first artificial plastic.

The word *plastic* covers a broad range of substances that all share the quality of being easily moldable. In fact, the word comes from the Greek *plastikos*, which means "fit for molding." Chemically speaking, plastics are organic polymers. These are very long chains of molecules, and it's this extraordinary length that gives polymers their peculiar bendy quality. The term *organic* in chemistry just means that a compound contains carbon, and most synthetic plastics get their carbon from petroleum, natural gas, or coal by-products. One of the qualities that earned praise for the first synthetic plastics is that they made good use of industrial waste. They were a green technology before the term *green technology* existed.

SYNTHESIZING A BETTER LIFE

To a nonscientist, the term *synthetic organic* might sound like a contradiction — but that's exactly the sort of substance most of us have in mind when we think of plastic. Hyatt's celluloid was derived from plant fiber, so it's at least seminatural. But the most quintessentially plasticky of plastics — stuff like garbage bags (polyethylene and polypropylene), Plexiglas (polymethyl methacrylate), and Styrofoam (polystyrene) — exist nowhere in nature. They are created in the laboratory.

The first of *that* kind of plastic was invented in 1907 in Yonkers, New York, by the Belgian-born chemist Leo Baekeland. This was not an act of pure, speculative science. Baekeland was just one of many scientists looking to exploit a market that had been created by celluloid.

Baekeland was searching for a synthetic wood varnish, but he came up with something much bigger — an artificial resin that was tough, lightweight, and resistant to heat and electricity. It was a perfect match for the times, when the home electronics industry was starting to take off. Baekeland's invention quickly began to appear in the form of casings for telephones, radios, and lamps, and in parts for irons, toasters, and automobiles.

The scientist-entrepreneur named this miracle substance *Bakelite*, after himself (which, from a marketing perspective, is much better than using its scientific name: polyoxybenzylmethylenglycolanhydride). Its logo was the mathematical symbol for infinity, and its slogan was "The Material of a Thousand Uses." (So it's safe to say that Baekeland understood the implications of his work.) By the time of his death, in 1944, Baekeland held more than 400 patents related to his invention, and his Bakelite Corp. factory took up 128 acres of industrial land in New Jersey. He left his heirs an extraordinary plastic fortune.

The breakaway success of Bakelite ushered in a host of competitors by the late 1920s. New formulations allowed these copycats to come in a wider variety of colors and even to be made translucent, to simulate amber, or to be marbled so as to look like, well, marble. Meanwhile, altogether new recipes for plastic were rapidly coming to market. Soon there was plastic jewelry, kitchenware, toys, chess pieces, domino and mah-jongg tiles, pipe stems and cigarette holders, bowling balls, buttons, airplane propellers, and eyeglass frames.

While the first commercial plastics mimicked luxury goods like tortoiseshell and ivory, plastic soon developed a cachet of its own — partially cultivated by savvy marketing from the plastics industry itself. Designers began producing high-end plastic furnishings — lamps and armchairs with

Lucite embellishments, serving dishes and cocktail shakers with Bakelite handles, aerodynamic clocks and radios for conspicuous display. At the peak of the Art Deco era, it was the height of chic to live in a streamlined wonderland of plastic, chrome, and glass.

Plastics were sexy and modern. A shining example of how science was improving the quality of everyday life, they became closely associated with exciting new technologies. Vinyl, for instance, was pressed into gramophone records and provided a more durable replacement to Edison's original wax cylinders, and celluloid found a new use as film stock for motion pictures. (It also was made into detachable men's collars that never lost their shape and saved consumers the expense of professional laundering and re-starching — a double win for modernity!)

From commercial success to cultural phenomenon, the natural next step was for plastic to grow into an ideology. In the conclusion to their book *Plastics*, British chemists Victor Yarsley and Edward Couzens envisioned a dawning era of safety, hygiene, convenience, and egalitarianism that would signify the pinnacle of human achievement: "Let us try to imagine a dweller in the 'Plastic Age,'" they wrote.

> This plastic man will come into a world of colour and bright shining surfaces where childish hands find nothing to break, no sharp edges, or corners to cut or graze, no crevices to harbour dirt or germs.... As he grows he cleans his teeth and brushes his hair with plastic brushes, clothes himself with in plastic clothes, writes his first lesson with a plastic pen and does his lessons in a book bound with plastic. The windows of his school curtained with plastic cloth entirely grease- and dirt- proof... and the frames, like those of his house are of moulded plastic, light and easy to open never requiring any paint.

In the autumn of his years, this man of the future "wears a denture with silent plastic teeth and spectacles with plastic lenses... until at last he sinks into his grave in a hygienically enclosed plastic coffin."

TO BUILD A DISPOSABLE DREAM

World War II was a catalyst for American manufacturing in general and plastics in particular. From 1940 to 1945, plastic production tripled from 310 million pounds to one billion pounds. Most all of it, however, was diverted to the war effort. What little went to civilian use was of poor quality — bowls that cracked and smelled funny, buttons that melted at the dry cleaner's — and the reputation of plastics began to decline.

But when the war ended, the plastics industry was ready to wage a public relations blitz on the home front. The era of the amateur chemist was over, and plastic was now in the hands of powerful and well-connected corporations like DuPont, Dow, Union Carbide, Standard Oil, and Monsanto. Backed by millions of dollars of investment from the Pentagon, plastic had become essential to national security and was an important sector of he economy. It was too big to fail.

To ensure it stayed that way, the industry eagerly sought out peacetime uses for its war-stimulated products. DuPont stared this process as early as 1943, even before D-day had swung the war decisively in the direction of the Allies. In April of 1946, just eight months after the Japanese surrender ended World War II, the plastics industry unveiled its new wares in a weeklong exposition in New York City. Fifteen thousand trade representatives attended, as did some 50,000 members of the general public. Accustomed to years of wartime rationing, visitors came to ogle a brave new world of conveniences and indulgences that were suddenly attainable. Shuffling past the booths of nearly 200 vendors, they were treated to displays of plastic window screens that never needed repainting; "run-proof" nylon stockings and no-starch treated cotton shirts; plastic contact lenses that invisibly corrected vision; plastic trumpets that needed no warming up; chip-resistant enamels to encase refrigerators, dishwashers, and washing machines. Teflon and silicone rubber, used extensively in the war, also made their public debut.

For those who couldn't attend in person, *House Beautiful* delivered its own take on the expo in the form of a 50-page insert titled "Plastics…A Way to a Better More Carefree Life."

This was all part of a concerted plan to maintain wartime levels of production and profit by increasing the appetite for plastic goods. The hook, however, wasn't opulence, as it had been before the war, but convenience,

THE GREAT PACIFIC GARBAGE PATCH

In 1997, skipper Charles Moore, returning to California after a boat race that had concluded in Hawaii, discovered a weird and unexplored region of the Pacific Ocean that was choked with plastic debris. In the week it took his boat, the *Alguita,* to cross this floating garbage dump, Moore was never out of sight of bottles, bottle caps, wrappers. But most of all, there were tiny shreds of plastic, so dense that they gave the water a soupy appearance.

Moore had discovered the Great Pacific Garbage Patch. Also known as the Pacific trash vortex, this vast accumulation of marine detritus is the product of a circular system of ocean currents called the North Pacific Subtropical Gyre, which spans the Pacific and flows clockwise from the equator up to around Vancouver, Canada, in the north.

Debris blown off the California coast and caught in the gyre will be swept down along Mexico and then out almost to Japan, where the Kuroshiro current will spin it back, down along the coast of the Pacific Northwest. Eventually, the trash tends to concentrate along the edges of the gyre, either in the vast garbage patch that Moore discovered between Hawaii and California or in a slightly smaller region close to Japan. This activity happens so far to the east that the trash vortex near California is called, somewhat confusingly, the Eastern Garbage Patch, while the one

novelty, and a bit of fun. A practical-minded style of shopping was being fostered — one that satisfied the ideals of the Puritan American work ethic while indulging our pleasure impulse as well. It allowed postwar consumers to gorge without getting a stomachache.

This virtuous spiral of consumption driving production, which then stimulates more consumption, sustained a booming economy. But there were dissenters to the new consensus. The chameleon face of plastic, poured and stretched into endless shapes for ever-growing purposes, inspired in many a new appreciation for the authentic — for the *organic*, not in the narrow chemical sense, but in what has since become the ordinary meaning: something natural and untampered with. Among the Beats and the hippies who followed them, *plastic* was never said without a snarl. This substance — cheap and disposable, conjured out of industrial waste, that could nearer Japan is the Western Garbage Patch.

Contrary to popular images, the trash vortices are not solid islands of garbage, and they're not entirely plastic either. Anything caught in the gyre will eventually congregate in the trash vortices, so oceanographers investigating the area have found all sorts of trash — semi-inflated beach balls and volleyballs, television picture tubes, truck tires, even barrels of toxic waste. However, since plastic does not biodegrade, it is the dominant pollutant.

While plastic does not decompose, sunlight does break it down into tiny pieces. So while there are scattered islands up to 50 feet long composed of discarded plastic products, countless tons more trash is in the form of fingernail-sized or smaller bits of plastic. That's what gives the waters of the region their soupy consistency.

And that's what poses one of the greatest environmental threats of the Pacific Garbage Patch. Feeding turtles and sea birds can mistake this plastic murk for jellyfish or roe. While it's not poisonous, plastic is, of course, not nutritious either and may be responsible for many animals starving to death. Moreover, the dense plastic layer reduces the amount of sunlight that penetrates the ocean, so it inhibits the growth of algae and plankton, which form the base of the marine food chain.

be anything but was itself nothing — came to represent a lifestyle predicated on wasteful abundance, where everything had a price but nothing had value.

A NEW NORMAL

By the early 1970s, it was not only possible but distressingly ordinary to see people leave their plastic-filled homes, clad entirely in plastic — from Dacron slacks to Ultrasuede jacket with rayon-nylon everywhere between — and strut their Naugahyde shoes across their Astroturf lawns. Yarsley and Couzens' prediction had in many ways come to pass. But this Plastic Age was far from what they had imagined in their frictionless, technocratic utopia. It was a garish nightmare born of unbound consumerism and an industry insulated from the consequences of its decisions.

One of those consequences was pollution. When the popular backlash against plastics came, it was not based on aesthetics or on a philosophical questioning of a life worth living. It came because plastic was posing an environmental threat that could no longer be ignored.

After half a century of widespread use, one overlooked quality of plastics suddenly became urgent: They don't decay. Each year, hundreds of thousands of tons of plastics were being dumped into landfills, where they just sat. The stuff that didn't make it to the dump was infiltrating the larger ecosystem. In 1960, plastic debris was first reported in the guts of seabirds. By the early 1970s, environmental awareness had gone mainstream, and reports of wildlife becoming entangled in plastic trash were finding a sympathetic audience.

These problems have only grown, as plastic now accounts for 28.5 million tons of trash each year, about 11 percent of everything we throw away. Beyond the impact on landfills and natural environments, there is a new concern that additives like PBA and DEHP, so-called plasticizers, could have toxic effects.

A survey from 2000 found that fewer than half of Americans had a positive opinion of plastic, and a quarter of us strongly believe that it does more harm than good. The heroic age of plastic is well and truly over. But like an addict now physically dependent on getting the next fix, quitting cold turkey is not an option.

Nor need it be. Like them or not, plastics are relatively energy efficient, requiring less energy to produce than the aluminum or glass they often replace. And while plastics are technically a petroleum product, their carbon stays trapped and is not released into the atmosphere like burnt fossil fuel. In many instances, plastics are simply our least-worst option. After all, who would argue that it's better to shoot an elephant for piano keys than to suffer with plastic?

So the eclipse of a former next big thing may point the way to the next next big thing. A hot topic in organic chemistry is the search for the next generation of plastics, ones that need no toxic additives and that will easily biodegrade. That might well signal a return to plant-based plastics, like celluloid — the discovery that started it all. ●

THE DANCE CRAZE

"Honey, honey, can't you hear
Funny, funny music, dear?…
Can't you see them all, swaying up the hall?…
Everybody's doin' it, doin' it, doin' it.
See that ragtime couple over there,
Watch them throw their shoulders in the air,
Snap their fingers, honey, I declare…
Everybody's doin' it now!"

— **IRVING BERLIN, FROM HIS SONG**
"EVERYBODY'S DOIN' IT," 1911

TIME OF ORIGIN: *1912*

ORIGIN IN: *New York*

HYPE FACTOR: *8 — You know how media pundits occasionally freak out about scandalous music and dance trends? Well, this was the first time it happened, so the freak-out was extra big.*

IMPACT FACTOR: *8 — This made dancing at clubs a respectable entertainment for every level of society and put black music right at the heart of American popular culture.*

Throughout the nineteenth century, America's elite took their cultural cues from Europe. And that extended to the way the 1 percent liked to party. Mansion ballrooms in all the best neighborhoods pulsed and swayed to the rhythms of languid waltzes composed by musicians from Germany, France, and England. But by the turn of the twentieth century, debutantes had begun to rebel against the stogy dance music that had already felt tired in their parents' day.

Quite unexpectedly, these bright young things turned to the syncopated sounds of ragtime, the house music of saloons and dance halls that had traditionally been forbidden to women of their elevated status. More scandalous still, they began *going out* to hear this music, to watch professionals dance to it, and even to try out the new steps themselves in the cabarets — forerunners of today's exclusive nightclubs — that began to dot Broadway in Midtown Manhattan and ruled the entertainment scene until World War I.

In these new pleasure palaces, the young and the old, the married and the single, all stampeded the floors to do the turkey trot, the grizzly bear, and the bunny hug in daring proximity to each other. A generation of Victorian constraint was abruptly dissolving into a barnyard bacchanal. And in this unlikely mingling of classes, races, and sexes, American popular culture was born.

GUARDIANS OF A FRACTURING CULTURE

From about 1890, ragtime music and the jazz dances that went with it started percolating up from black saloons in the South. Through New Orleans bordellos, Texas honky-tonks, and dive bars on San Francisco's Barbary Coast, they reached the vast melting pot of New York by 1911, and from there went viral. As with rock 'n' roll 50 years later, an African American musical form was adapted by the white, often Jewish, songwriters of Tin Pan Alley for a mass audience. Meanwhile, touring exhibition dancers brought the cakewalk and its cousins to white audiences in theaters on the vaudeville circuit.

But excitement over the new dance styles became a genuine craze in 1912, when exhibition dancers Irene and Vernon Castle returned to the US from a triumphal season in Paris. They had left New York a year earlier complete unknowns, but European audiences enthusiastically embraced the couple's presentation of the colorful and modern American dances. Having received the imprimatur of European tastemakers, jazz dance was now acceptable in even the highest levels of American society. And the Castles, the unofficial jazz ambassadors to France, would be the ones to teach the two-step to America's blue bloods.

In 1913, the couple, dubbed the "Society Dancers," opened Castle House across from the Ritz-Carlton Hotel. From there, the Castles presided like hosts at a private ball. Irene, in particular, became the voice and face of the respectable modern dancer. Young, pretty, and refined, she embodied the new freedoms women were enjoying — both in and outside the cabarets — and made them unthreatening. While Americans had once idealized women in their role as mothers, Irene Castle and the other so-called New Women of this era were introducing a new feminine ideal of beautiful and carefree youth. For good and for ill, it's an ideal that still endures.

A REVOLUTION IN MOTION

One by one, the opulent hotels and gaudy lobster palaces of Fifth Avenue started laying down dance floors. Maxim's, Rector's, Churchill's, and Murray's offered not just cabaret shows and dancing at night but also afternoon tea dances, where, for a few dollars, an unchaperoned woman, young or old, housewife or shopgirl, could hire

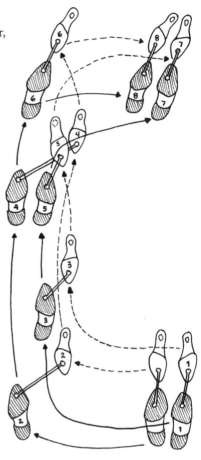

a dance partner to teach her the latest steps or simply to twirl her around the floor. By the early 1910s, it was possible, and even acceptable, to dance from nearly one dawn to the next.

That was an enormous change over a shockingly brief time.

The freedom to dance at whim had previously been available at only the lowest level of society, in the saloons and dance halls of red-light districts. The people at the apex of the social pyramid concentrated their dancing in the winter social season and confined it to formal balls in private homes.

Social dances, like the German and the lancer, put a heavy emphasis on the *social*, for their elaborate figures and frequent partner changes (think of a refined and restrained square dance) discouraged intimacy by engaging everyone on the dance floor. Even in closed-hold dances, such as the waltz, where the man held the woman at the waist in a semi-embrace, dancers maintained a respectable distance from each other — four inches at the shoulders — and dared not be seen with the same partner too often, a faux pas of overeagerness that was avoided by the custom of filling out a dance card.

The new dances, on the other hand, were utterly informal. And with their simple, walk-like steps, they struck many as simplistic and monotonous. But where they completely broke with tradition was above the feet: From swiveling hips to shaking shoulders and flailing limbs, dancers' entire bodes were now in unrestrained and unscripted motion. To dance to the music, you needed to *feel* the music.

INEVITABLE REACTION

As dancing waxed from popular pastime to full-fledged obsession, moralists of all stripes began to take disapproving notice. Traditionalists, who wanted to see women consigned to the home, and progressives, who thought they should be allowed to have the vote and pursue careers, could both agree on one point: Alcohol and riotous dancing was bad for anyone — but particularly for the fairer sex. To these scolds, the spectacle of women moving their bodies uninhibitedly and mingling freely in public and among strangers represented a deplorable debasement of femininity that was a threat to civilization itself.

Behind the condescending paternalism lurked the bile of racial hatred. One particular editorial for the *New York World* — nasty in tone but typical in sentiment — fulminated against "obscene cannibalistic dances… animalistic and vile and redolent of the Negro in his most bestial activities and blood sacrificial rites. They are voodoo; they were once taboo; and now our women dance them with all who come!"

Not that race mixing was even happening in the cabarets: The only African Americans in them were entertainers, not patrons. But for critics, the music and the dances themselves were fruit of a poison tree: No matter who danced them, no matter where they were danced, and no matter how much they were whitewashed — nothing could redeem them from their tainted origins in African American culture.

THE ORIGINAL TWERKERS

No dance caused more controversy than the tango, the sensual Argentine dance traditionally accompanied by the accordion-like bandoneon. From South America, it spread first to Paris and then the rest of the world, inciting passion wherever it went. By 1913, the international scandal had reached American shores: When Yale banned the dance from its junior prom, it made front-page news; when Harvard announced that it *would* tango, that was even bigger news.

Society dames were divided: Some publicly denounced the tango, refusing to allow it in their homes and even forming committees to have it banned; others, such as Mrs. John Astor, hosted their own tango parties, and Elsie de Wolfe, an influential interior designer and arbiter of taste, took a firm stand and defended the dance as "chaste" and "refined."

In Italy, the Duke of Abruzzi was blamed for corrupting Italian society when he allowed the tango at his villa. The King of Bavaria forbade all military officers from participating in any festivity at which it was danced. However, England's dowdy Queen Mary enjoyed watching Maurice Mouvet execute the tango's complex movements.

Physicians condemned the tango for causing a host of illnesses, from tango foot to fallen stomach to "overstimulation," even, in one case, blaming it for a dancer's death. The Vatican declared the tango immoral, its practitioners sinful; bishops around the world banished it from their dioceses. One Italian cardinal branded the dance "revolting and disgusting," although it was reported that the pope himself was more tolerant: After watching the dance, he observed wryly that if the tango were a penance, people would regard it as sheer cruelty.

The ire directed at the tango was, to a degree, misdirected. When danced correctly, the tango was in some respects more modest than other new dances, with partners dancing side by side rather than facing each other, and engaging in little physical contact.

Not many amateurs danced it correctly, however, and *tango* came to be used as an umbrella term for modern, lascivious dances. A report filed by a volunteer operative of New York City's semi-official morality police, the Committee of Fourteen, describes what many imagined about the tango:

On the floor among the dancers were a young girl and a man of about fifty, who were both totally drunk, so much so that they could scarcely keep their feet and were constantly bumping into other couples. The man was bending the girl over backward and pressing her body close to his and placing his knee between her legs and was feeling her thighs with his right hand.… They simply pivoted round in a small corner of the dancing space going through the above gyrations.

APPROPRIATION

Professional exhibition dancers refined the tango, toning down its sensuality, just as they had with the African American dances. Deliberately obscuring its Caribbean-slave origins and long incubation in the seedier quarters of Buenos Aires, the Castles suggested that it had originated in Spain and emphasized that they danced the *Parisian* tango. One academician actually argued that the dance had been passed down from classical antiquity.

In America's first popular-dance craze, we can see the template for every pop cultural phenomenon to follow: A new art form trickles up from the cultural margins; traditionalists then balk and use it as an opportunity to vent their paranoia about race relations, changing sexual mores, and degenerating cultural standards; meanwhile, popularizers, opportunists, and even sincere second-wave fans arrive, diluting the trend and rendering it accessible and bland enough for mass appeal; and the cultural adventurers move on to search for the next big thing.

There's no denying that ragtime was whitewashed, or that high-toned cabarets replaced black musicians with white ones as soon as there was a deep enough talent pool. Nevertheless, the dance craze opened up America to its diverse cultures; and whether the mainstream could acknowledge it or not, black music was now embedded in American popular culture.

Soon records, radio, and movies would disseminate a new national culture, and that culture would be less focused on Europe and less fixated on high art. Popular music would now be primarily dance music, and tastemakers would go looking to the streets, not the parlors of the elite. ●

THE TEENAGER

"Hey Johnny, what are you rebelling against?"
"Whaddaya got?"

— MILDRED (PEGGY MALEY) AND JOHNNY
(MARLON BRANDO) IN *THE WILD ONE*, 1953

TIME OF ORIGIN: *Late 1930s*

ORIGIN IN: Seventeen *magazine and other media outlets*

HYPE FACTOR: *9 — The teenage ideal had hardly been defined when authority figures were already lamenting what a disappointing menace teens actually were.*

IMPACT FACTOR: *9 — In less than 100 years, teens have gone from nonexistence to assuming a cultural and economic dominance.*

Although the giddy anguish (or is it anguished giddiness?) of adolescence may well be as ancient as our species itself, the *teenager* is a historical phenomenon — a media and marketing creation made possible by two factors: the rapid growth in high school attendance in the first half of the twentieth century and the post–World War II prosperity that put generous allowance money into the pockets of the nation's adolescents.

Before the war, parents and older kids liked pretty much the same stuff, wore more or less the same clothes, and listened to the same music. Sure, individuals might prefer jazz or classical or country, but age wasn't a demographic factor here — not one that anybody had noticed yet, at any rate. Once segregated onto high school campuses, however, the nation's adolescents started to develop their own trends and tastes that were inscrutable to adult sensibilities. What teens liked became "cool," and once business became aware of the economic power of this new cohort, it was happy to package cool and sell it back to teens.

Once that dynamic began, the longevity of the teenager was guaranteed. Uncomprehending parents might protest the bizarre antics of their teens, but from an commercial standpoint this new demographic could do no wrong.

THE BIRTH OF THE TEENAGER

For most of human history, the presence of a culturally sanctioned space where children could be gently shepherded into adulthood was a luxury reserved for the elite. For the vast poor majority, childhood ended and adulthood began as soon as a person was able to labor — either out in the fields or back at home, cooking and keeping house.

One of the consequences of the nineteenth-century industrial revolution, however, was a twentieth-century job market that required greater training and education. Instead of going to straight work, more and more not-quite-adults started going to school. In 1910, just 15 percent of US teens attended high school; 20 years later, almost half did. In 1940, a majority of 17-year-olds would earn a high school diploma. This movement out of the workplace and into the classroom produced widespread cultural ripples as tens of thousands of adolescents who would have been quietly absorbed into the world of grownup responsibilities were now enjoying the semi-leisured, quasi adulthood of high school life.

THE TEEN PROTOTYPE

Even as high school classrooms were swelling, a changing approach to education and child development started to emphasize moral as well as academic growth. School became a place to instill pro-social, middle-class values in the motley assortment of ethnic, immigrant, and working-class kids now vying for a high school diploma. But the prevailing pedagogical outlook was surprisingly tolerant and optimistic: Though plagued by temptations and eager to assert their independence, adolescents, it was thought, were primarily wholesome and fun-loving scamps who secretly craved guidance and rules — if gently applied — and did not balk at the idea of growing up and conforming to societal expectations.

It was this comforting myth that shaped early images of teenagers that emerged in the late 1930s and lingers to this day in the figure of the preppy:

blond-haired girls in prim sweater sets or androgynous sweatshirts; freckle-faced boys in pressed khakis and letterman jackets or woolly blazers. For the real-life models behind this proto-teen image — the children of the moneyed, professional class — high school was indeed prep school. While they might spend afternoons at the drugstore soda bar dancing to swing tunes on the jukebox, these young lions were eager to toe the line and assume their adult roles on Wall Street or in politics, as a country doctor or small-town lawyer, or as a wife and society dame. With its student-body elections and clubs and elaborate social pecking order, high school was a microcosm of the upper-middle-class adult world, its homecomings and cotillions mirroring the country club rituals of the Establishment.

By 1941, when the word *teenager* first starts being used in the way we know it today, this image of the high school student was already an anachronism, but it nonetheless remained a powerful role model. And it was bolstered by a small but growing body of morally edifying entertainment aimed at teens. In the pages of *Seventeen* and *Scholastic* magazines; in teen fiction, such as the Hardy Boys and Nancy Drew mystery novels; and in the 15 Andy Hardy movies released between 1937 and 1946, in which actor Mickey Rooney embodied America's quintessential teen, upwardly mobile adolescents were bombarded with well-curated tableaux of middle-class mores for them to emulate.

But as a nation of concerned parents would soon learn, cultural influence can work both ways.

TEEN 2.0: THE REBEL

As high school attendance became nearly universal, the small preppy elite was no longer able to define the high school experience. Despite educators' hope that more schooling would bring more people into the bourgeoisie fold, high schools became an equally effective network for spreading dissenting attitudes. For every striver who aimed to become the first college grad in the family, there was a middle-class hipster who adopted street styles and slang as a gesture of provocation or a bid for authenticity.

This "trickle-up" phenomenon was first fully demonstrated in the rock 'n' roll explosion of the 1950s. In urban areas throughout the nation, a strain of rhythm and blues with a danceable beat and often suggestive lyrics had attained a cult status among teens in the late '40 and early '50s. In a pattern that has not been broken to this day, entrepreneurs with a finger on the teen pulse spotted the trend, cleaned it up, hyped it, and cashed in. [See **Rock 'n' Roll**]

Unlike the earlier teen-oriented products, which were created by adults with the ulterior motive of character building, the rock 'n' roll trend just followed teen taste and aimed to indulge it. It was the first expression of a genuine teenage subculture.

Predictably, the adult reaction was unbridled hysteria. Rock 'n' roll was the music of African Americans and of poor whites from the inner cities and the Deep South. Working class, unbridled, disrespectful, pleasure seeking, it represented everything that was supposed to be walled out of the high school campus — which is exactly why teens dug it so much.

While parents clung to preppy fantasies, the kids were entranced by hoodlums and rebels, like those immortalized on the screen by Marlon Brando and James Dean in movies like *The Wild Ones* and *Rebel Without a Cause* — tough but sensitive, romantically destined to lose but never to bend.

THE ENDLESS QUEST FOR THE AUTHENTIC

The rebel is an apt image for the teenager. Adolescence is a time of experimentation and self-discovery. And more often than not that discovery unfolds as a series of negative revelations: I'm *not* my parents; I'm *not* a child; I'm *not* a nerd; I'm *not* a jock. The question of what one *is*, though, remains hazy and tentative, and thus open to influence from all sides.

That adolescence is short-lived and seeks to express its uniqueness through what it rejects all but guarantees that there will never be an end to what teenagers can be sold. But there is particular tension built into the phenomenon of teenager from the start. On one hand is the incessant desire to find an authentic expression of adolescent identity; on the other is an equally dogged pressure to find that expression through purchasing decisions. "Buy this, and you will be cool" has always been the sales pitch to teenagers. And they always turn to look for something else, something real — which is quickly packaged and sold to them.

This cat-and-mouse dynamic of cool-hunting has been a dominant engine of culture and commerce ever since it first played out in the 1950s. ●

HISTORIC YOUTH SUBCULTURES

Because of the role youth has played in shaping culture for almost a century now, youth subcultures appear throughout this book. Hippies and mods, B-boys and fly girls, glam rockers and ravers — whatever ideas united them, they all signaled their tribal identity through music and dress. The glut of downloading and streaming options has tended to devalue music as an identity marker in the Internet age, and to take its place other affiliations and interests have stepped up — whether they be comic books and cosplay, taxidermy and Victorian science, gaming, or My Pretty Pony. Youth subculture is far from over, but the character has changed from the golden era of music-driven style tribes.

Here are a few classic subcultures that don't show up in other sections but deserve a mention.

TEDDY BOY

ORIGIN: *England, 1950s*

One of the first youth subcultures to be named embodied a British take on American rock 'n' roll; its members also shared a taste for burlesque-club jazz and a rock-like form of roots music called skiffle. Teddy boys grew long sideburns and combed their hair into greasy pompadours, much like American rockers (with whom they also shared a reputation for violence and hooliganism), but they wore a distinctively British look: long frock coats with velvet collars, flashy brocade vests, and narrow drainpipe trousers. It's this neo-Edwardian style that gave the group their name, teddy boys.

ESSENTIAL TRACKS:
"The Creep," Ken Mackintosh, 1953
"Rock Island Line," Lonnie Donegan, 1954
"Be-Bop-A-Lula," Gene Vincent, 1956
"C'mon Everybody," Eddie Cochran, 1958

HEAVY METAL

ORIGIN: *Birmingham, England, home to Black Sabbath, 1970*

Spurned even within the countercultural world of high school rejects, heavy metal never has gotten any respect. The term was coined by hard rock act Steppenwolf in the 1968 classic "Born to Be Wild," but the song was more a call to action than a template for the heavy metal sound. Steppenwolf's challenge was taken up in the UK by bands like Led Zeppelin, Jethro Tull, and, especially, Black Sabbath, who combined electric rock with heavy blues and a faerie-dust sprinkling of ye olde England folk imagery that quickly turned into horror-movie deviltry. When the lighter and more rollicking glam sound swept Britain in the early '70s, America took up the metal mantle, and for more than two decades it served as the anthem for the unrepentantly adolescent white American male, reaching its pinnacle (or nadir) in the Satan-praising, party-loving hair bands of the 1980s.

Say what you will, though, metal is still the perfect soundtrack for gaming, whether you prefer an Xbox or old-fashioned paper and polyhedron dice.

ESSENTIAL ALBUMS:

Paranoid, Black Sabbath, 1970
British Steel, Judas Priest, 1980
Ace of Spades, Motörhead, 1981
Reign in Blood, Slayer, 1986
Master of Puppets, Metallica, 1986

PUNK

ORIGIN: *CBGB bar, New York, 1974*

The excesses of the 1960s left the nation with a rash of drug deaths, rising rates of addiction, and an epidemic of teenage runaways. The economy was stagnating and crime was growing. No place was hit harder than New York City, which was teetering on the edge of bankruptcy. But in the desperate Lower East Side at a dingy club called CBGB, a set of urban bohemians was turning adversity into art.

Responding to a similar cultural and economic malaise, the UK quickly devised its own version of punk, which jettisoned the avant-garde pretensions of its American cousin in favor of a more stridently political and working-class sensibility. On the other hand, fashion played more of a role there than here. While American punks were mostly shabby and understated in Levi's 501s and decal T-shirts, British punks peacocked in tartan "bondage pants," distressed mohair sweaters, and torn and safety-pinned vintage jackets, and popularized the brilliantly dyed Mohawk haircut.

The sartorial excess was no accident. The great British punk impresario Malcolm McLaren, who managed the legendary Sex Pistols and did much to define the London scene, was the business and romantic partner of designer Vivienne Westwood, who now makes couture gowns for pop stars and royalty.

ESSENTIAL ALBUMS, US:

 Horses, Patti Smith, 1975

 The Ramones, the Ramones, 1976

 Marquee Moon, Television, 1977

 Blank Generation, Richard Hell and the Voidoids, 1977

ESSENTIAL ALBUMS, UK:

 Damned Damned Damned, the Damned, 1977

 The Clash, the Clash, 1977

 Never Mind the Bollocks, Here's the Sex Pistols, Sex Pistols, 1977

 A Different Kind of Tension, Buzzcocks, 1979

GOTH

ORIGIN: *The Batcave club, London, 1982*

While American rock has always been heavy on ego and rebellious aggression, British rock has a deep strain of theatrical escapism. As punk became more violent and politically doctrinaire, a backlash set in. The most extreme form was the goth subculture, which combined the flamboyance of glam, a touch of hippie new ageism, and a fascination with kinky sexuality, all wrapped up in a dark-eyeliner-and-black-velvet horror movie look culled from the silent classics *Nosferatu* and *The Cabinet of Dr. Caligari* down through the schlocky Hammer films of the 1960s and early '70s.

ESSENTIAL LISTENING:

Juju, Siouxsie and the Banshees, 1981
"Bela Lugosi's Dead," Bauhaus, 1982
Pornography, the Cure, 1982
First and Last and Always, the Sisters of Mercy, 1985

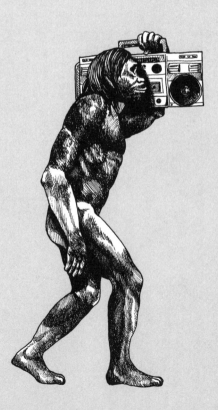

GRUNGE AND RIOT GRRRL
ORIGIN: *Pacific Northwest, 1990*

In the late '70s and through the '80s, the US record industry mostly ignored punk and the alternative music that followed in its wake. But it made up for this oversight by pouncing on the Seattle-area music scene that was hitting its stride in the early '90s. The destructive effects of too much fame too soon are encapsulated in the drug- and depression-related suicide of Nirvana front man Kurt Cobain. While it's a matter of debate how much the bands labeled as grunge shared in common and how much they differed from the typical alternative rock of the late '80s, there's no disagreement that grunge marked the moment when the underground went mainstream.

On the other hand, the loosely associated riot grrrl movement managed to keep its indie credibility — largely because the self-consciously dorky look of the bands and their prickly but uproarious feminist message did nothing to court commercial success. All that, however, did win enthusiastic support among college students, and the riot grrrl influence — both in fashion and gender politics — can still be seen in today's hipsters.

ESSENTIAL ALBUMS, GRUNGE:
Superfuzz Bigmuff, Mudhoney, 1988
Bleach, Nirvana, 1989
Ten, Pearl Jam, 1991
Badmotorfinger, Soundgarden, 1991

ESSENTIAL LISTENING, RIOT GRRRL:
"Hate My Way," Throwing Muses, 1986
Bricks Are Heavy, L7, 1992
Pussy Whipped, Bikini Kill, 1993
Pottymouth, Bratmobile, 1993
Call the Doctor, Sleater-Kinney, 1996

ROCK 'N' ROLL

"Man, we're the first generation in history to have a music all our own!"

— TEENAGE AUDIENCE MEMBER AT ALAN
FREED'S ROCK 'N' ROLL REVUE, 1957

TIME OF ORIGIN: *1951*

ORIGIN IN: *Cleveland*

HYPE FACTOR: *10 — Combine equal parts teenagers, sex, and rebellion, add a pinch of race mixing and stir well. Add directly into the deep-fat fryer of 1950s America, and you have a foolproof recipe for a cultural bombe surprise.*

IMPACT FACTOR: *8 — The very name rock 'n' roll was a media creation, but it tapped into a genuine hunger in the youth market for a distinctive sound and a safe way to rebel.*

Rock 'n' roll is king. Even if you've never heard of Chuck Berry and can't tell Little Richard from the Big Bopper, you are indebted to them. Rock 'n' roll is part of all Americans; it's woven into our pop culture DNA. The very notion of pop culture — cheap, flashy, ephemeral, with proudly vulgar flouting of respectability and good taste — grew to ascendancy in the rock 'n' roll era. The sounds have changed, but we still haven't exited the era.

THE TRANQUILIZER GENERATION

As 1950 kicked over into 1951, a snoozy single called "The Tennessee Waltz" was in the middle of a 30-week stay on the Top 40 chart. With a delivery that is languid to the point of comatose, the singer, Patti Page, laments the song — the eponymous Tennessee Waltz — that has brought together her lover and her old friend in a budding romance, leaving the mournful singer (as the listener can only conclude) alone and heavily sedated at a sanitarium somewhere in the Appalachians.

Mawkish, complacent, and all but impossible for anyone with a pulse to dance to, "The Tennessee Waltz" is truly unbearable. But it was by no means an outlier for its time, when the charts were dominated by slow-tempo, lushly orchestrated ballads by late-era crooners, like Nat King Cole and Perry Como. Sonically, it was as though the nation had downed a bottle of tranquilizers.

Which is exactly what the grown-ups wanted. Dads, haunted by the memories of the death camps and jungle warfare of World War II, found numbing relief in martinis and the anonymity of corporate culture, while moms, experiencing the benefits of new consumer appliances like dishwashers and washing machines, now had enough leisure time to finally catch their breath and realize what a crushing grind homemaking was. Barbiturates helped. So did Patti Page.

But in July 1951, a much-needed shot of adrenaline would be delivered into the nation's jugular. On Cleveland's WJW radio, a DJ named Alan Freed put away his classical records and started spinning contemporary rhythm and blues tracks, which he dubbed "rock 'n' roll." Styling himself as "the King of all Moondoggers," Freed would banter in a manic stream of hep talk, howl and shout his approval over songs, and occasionally pop open a beer.

The kids heard. And there was dancing again.

STIRRINGS FROM BELOW

The backstory of rock 'n' roll reveals a classically American blend of opportunism, corruption, and genuine evangelical zeal.

The economic boom that followed World War II was truly a tide that lifted all boats. In 1950, the average African American worker was earning four times what he'd been making in 1940. The African American population living on farms plummeted from 35 percent to 8 percent, as some three million left the Deep South for northern cities.

Newly prospering African Americans represented a significant untapped market, and marketers were quick to act. In 1948, WDIA in Memphis ditched its pop music format to become the nation's first black-oriented

ROCK 'N' ROLL HONOR ROLL

"Rocket 88," by Jackie Brenston and his Delta Cats, 1951. It was a gradual transformation that turned the boogie-woogie of the 1930s into the jump blues of the 1940s and the rock 'n' roll of the 1950s. While music obsessives agree on what rock 'n' roll is — 12-bar blues structure, heavy emphasis on the two and four beats, and a minimalist ensemble of drum, bass, saxophone or electric guitar, and sometimes piano — there is no consensus on when these elements first came together on vinyl. While precursors can be spotted as far back as the mid-1940s, most fans, however, accept that "Rocket 88" has all the requisite pieces — plus it features a distorted guitar sound (the accidental effect of a torn amp) that helped define the rock sound.

"Rock Around the Clock," by Bill Haley and the Comets, 1955. "Rock Around the Clock" wasn't the first rock 'n' roll hit, but it was the first sensation. Recorded in 1954, the single didn't catch on until it was used in the movie *Blackboard Jungle*, a film offering a gritty look at an urban high school that was intended as a scathing indictment of juvenile delinquent culture. What teen audiences saw instead was the prototype of the rock 'n' roll rebel, the born-to-lose antihero who still embodies the spirit of rock. "Rock Around the Clock" became a teen anthem, a defiant declaration of intent.

radio station. By the mid-'50s, 21 other stations had done the same, and more than 600 others had at least some "Negro-slanted" programming.

With vastly increased radio play, African American performers had greater opportunities to release records. The sound was rhythm and blues, a direct descendent of 1930s boogie-woogie, but with a heavy, loping back-beat that made it irresistible for dancing. In segregated America, the major labels were not interested in what they dismissively branded "race music," but smaller, independent labels were happy to take over the rhythm and blues market. They paid poorly and were, not infrequently, downright exploitive of their artists, but the indie labels ushered in a golden age of black music.

"Maybellene," by Chuck Berry, 1955. Saxophone and piano were the signature sounds of early rock 'n' roll, but they would be displaced by the electric guitar. One of the first artists to push the instrument into prominence was Chuck Berry. His distorted electric guitar intro to "Maybellene" — though only a few seconds long — is a revelation of the creative potential of sheer noise.

"Heartbreak Hotel," by Elvis Presley, 1956. The greatest artists transcend their genre. Elvis would be crowned the King, but many at first disputed his place in rock 'n' roll — including Alan Freed, the man who coined the term himself. Classic rock 'n' roll descended directly from the rhythm and blues that was coming out of cities like Chicago, Memphis, New York, and Los Angeles. But Elvis was making a country-R&B hybrid called, often derisively, *rockabilly*. He wasn't the only one — many white rock acts, including superstar Bill Haley, were playing rockabilly. But in Elvis's case, both the black and the hillbilly elements were supercharged, which alienated many listeners. Even while he was garnering a loyal audience through touring, Elvis had difficulty breaking through on radio: White stations thought he sounded too black, and black stations thought he was too country. "Heartbreak Hotel," a darkly brooding single that erupts into sudden lacerating guitar riffs, is almost more a blues song than rock. It became Elvis's first number one hit.

Nevertheless, in the late '40s and early '50s, rhythm and blues records formed only a niche market. They didn't chart on the Top 40, they didn't get played on white radio, and — worst of all — they didn't sell to white consumers.

THE ROCK 'N' ROLL PROPHET

Alan Freed had been a DJ for nearly a decade playing various formats at various stations when he was approached by Leo Mintz, the owner of a record shop on the edge of Cleveland's inner city that was popular with white and black clientele. Mintz was puzzling out a dilemma: The white kids were digging the up-tempo R&B records Mintz was playing at his store, but they weren't buying them. Mintz, like hundreds of other record store owners and radio station managers across the country, was confronting the barrier of entrenched racial prejudice.

What Mintz suggested was that Freed play this new music and make it acceptable to a white audience. Mintz would sponsor the show, and they'd both get rich.

Freed was initially skeptical. But a visit to Mintz's store convinced him that they were on to something big. It was electrifying for Freed to see these entertainment-starved teens circumventing the cultural gatekeepers and creating a scene for themselves — an exclusive teen subculture within the gray-flannel drabness of the mainstream '50s.

Within a week, classical was out of Freed's playlist and race music was in — under the more palatable moniker *rock 'n' roll*, an expression that had been bouncing around the R&B world for years and was both an apt description of the new syncopated, beat-heavy sound and an unsubtle double entendre that would please the kids and rattle the squares.

BACKLASH TO THE BACKBEAT

Freed was right on both counts. The kids flocked to rock 'n' roll, while the adults were eager to attack it. Defending the musical status quo in 1957, crooner Frank Sinatra blasted rock 'n' roll as "a rancid smelling aphrodisiac." He was echoing the sentiments of countless parents when he continued, "It is sung, played, and written for the most part by cretinous goons, and by means of its imbecilic reiteration and sly, lewd, in plain fact dirty, lyrics it manages to be the martial music of every sideburned delinquent on the face of the earth."

Sinatra's broadside was colorful, but it was by no means the nastiest criticism. From *Time* magazine to the *New York Times*, the media condemned the new music, often branding it as "tribal," "cannibalistic," "jungle music," and leveling other not-so-thinly-veiled racist jibes at it.

ROCK IS DEAD; LONG LIVE ROCK 'N' ROLL!

In 1954, Alan Freed left Cleveland for New York, and rock 'n' roll grew from youth cult into national phenomenon. Freed started producing rock concerts, TV shows, and even series of schlocky rock 'n' roll-themed movies. He was cashing in, but he remained an outspoken advocate for teen culture.

But revolutions last only so long. By the late '50s, the major labels had stopped resisting and jumped aboard the rock 'n' roll bandwagon. The result was a glut of sanitized white rock acts, saccharine teen idols, and bland cover versions of hard-rocking songs.

Meanwhile, corruption at the heart of the music industry was exposed when the payola scandal broke in 1959. It was revealed that a number of high-profile DJs had been improperly receiving music royalties and other financial inducements to promote certain rock 'n' roll singles. Freed was among the tainted DJs, and his was the first head to roll. In 1959, his career was effectively over. Alcoholic and increasingly isolated, the Godfather of Rock 'n' Roll died in 1965.

But by then rock 'n' roll was already dead as well. Sideburn-wearing greasers from Memphis and gold-lamé-clad strutters from Chicago weren't getting records cut and couldn't sell them even when they did. The first generation of rockers had aged out of adolescence, and their younger siblings were now swinging to the British beat of the Beatles and the Rolling Stones.

Rock 'n' roll was over — but rock music lived on, as it still does, with ever-changing looks and sounds, but always feeding that same teenage craving for a community of fellow rebels. ●

3-D MOVIES

"A LION in your lap! A LOVER in your arms!"

— *BWANA DEVIL* PROMO, 1952

TIME OF ORIGIN: *1952*

ORIGIN IN: *The motion picture* Bwana Devil

HYPE FACTOR: *4 — Sure, it was hyped at the time, but there was so much hype in the '50s that 3-D barely stood out.*

IMPACT FACTOR: *1 — The original 3-D technology did nothing to change moviemaking or storytelling. So far, 3-D version 2.0 hasn't had any effect either.*

For years, the 1950s were remembered for their fads. There was Hula-Hooping and hot-rodding, for instance. There were also poodle skirts. (If you've never heard of them, a poodle skirt is a loose, brightly colored skirt… with a poodle patch on it.)

But one of the most derided trends was a gimmick called the 3-D movie. Imagine — people used to think in the '60s, '70s, '80s, and '90s — watching a whole movie with a ridiculous pair of cardboard glasses on your head! Wouldn't you get a headache? Wouldn't you get motion sickness? Could the illusion of depth really make yet another schlocky fantasy-adventure movie any better?

But since the 2000s, scoffers have had ample opportunity to find out for themselves, as Hollywood again rallied behind this 1950s novelty. And it did so for the same reason it did the first time: slumping ticket sales.

THE GOLDEN AGE OF 3-D: 1952–1955

In 1946, more than 78 million Americans went to the movies at least once a week. By 1951, that number had dropped to under 55 million. Many factors were at play, but movie studios put the blame squarely on a new form of competition: television. In 1946, fewer than one of every 200 US homes had a TV set, but by 1951 the number was almost one in four. Three years later, more than 55 percent of American homes had a TV.

An alarmed movie industry responded by offering experiences that could not be matched at home. One of them was 3-D.

Bwana Devil, a low-budget adventure yarn set in deepest, darkest Africa (but filmed in Malibu), was not exactly the first 3-D film — they'd been around since the '20s. But it was the first color, dual-strip, 3-D Polaroid movie. Technicalities aside, *Bwana Devil* is important because it was the movie that started the first sustained period of 3-D filmmaking.

In the popular imagination, 3-D movies were plot-light pastiches of flinch-inducing gestures that threatened to break right out of the flat theater screen: cowboys hawking tobacco spit, and savage Indians shooting flaming arrows into the audience; madmen wielding scalpels; gangsters waving glowing cigars; buxom beauties hurtling splashfully into vats of molten wax.

Yes, there was plenty of all that. But the popular imagination was only partially correct.

Approximately 45 3-D features were released during the novelty's so-called golden age — and not all of them were cheap kids' shows. Venerated Broadway composer Cole Porter had a stereoscopic release of *Kiss Me Kate* (1953), his musical take on Shakespeare's *The Taming of the Shrew*. Cowboy actor John Wayne, one of the biggest stars of the time, also starred in a well-received 3-D film, *Hondo* (1953). In 1954, suspense director Alfred Hitchcock jumped on the bandwagon with *Dial M for Murder*. But by then, however, the 3-D wave had crested, and the film fared better in traditional 2-D format.

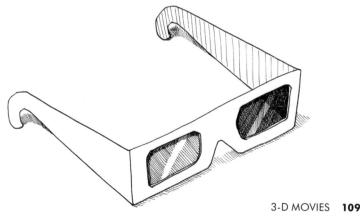

CAPTURING THE THIRD DIMENSION

Like a camera, each of our eyes sees in just two dimensions. Our ability to perceive depth is the result of our two eyes being conveniently separated by our nose. Because of this displacement, the image each eye receives is slightly different. When the brain resolves the images, two dimensions become three. Three-dimensional cinematography works the same way.

The typical 3-D movie was shot using two cameras that were actually facing each other. Angled mirrors directed the light from the scene into each lens. If that sounds unwieldy, check out how projection worked.

Showing a 3-D movie required two projectors that had to be exactly aligned and perfectly synchronized. Being off by as little as one eighth of a frame could cause eyestrain; slippage by a full frame would ruin image quality as well.

To separate the now-superimposed images so that each eye would see just the reel meant for it, each projector was fitted with a screen that polarized the light. Polarized glasses that the audience wore filtered the light to admit just the correct image.

CLOSED FOR TECHNICAL DIFFICULTIES

After the novelty faded, audiences were tepid about 3-D. Nevertheless, the technology might have survived — if theaters and projectionist hadn't loathed it.

Contrary to conventional wisdom, it wasn't the quality of 3-D movies that drove them to extinction; it was the quality of the technology. It took two projectors to show a 3-D film — one playing a strip for the right eye, and one the other for the left – and if the two strips were even minutely out of sync, audiences could suffer eyestrain and motion sickness.

In 1953, the biblical epic *The Robe* debuted a new process called CinemaScope. The selling point here was a widescreen format almost twice as broad as that of other films, and big sound to match, in the form of new stereophonic audio. Cinemascope was every bit as spectacular as 3-D, but without the technical frustrations.

The response was decisive: One month after *The Robe* opened, the last studio 3-D film went into production, and 3-D screenings for 1954 were drastically scaled back. *Revenge of the Creature*, a sequel to *The Creature from the Black Lagoon*, was the only 3-D film released in 1955. The fad was over.

3-D REDUX

A brief, campy revival of 3-D in the '80s (anyone remember *Jaws 3-D?*) seemed only to prove that stereoscopic cinema was over as anything other than a joke.

In the twenty-first century, though, Hollywood has had little to laugh about. For the past ten years, ticket sales in the US and Canada have hovered at just over one billion admissions annually. Any rise in profit has come solely from raising the price of tickets — and the added experience of new 3-D is a justification to charge more.

But is the new 3-D more than cynical marketing? The critical and box-office success of 2013's *Gravity* shows what can happen when good storytelling is combined with innovative special effects. The next few years may well prove whether our current 3-D age will be remembered for its *Hondo*s and *Kiss Me Kate*s or for its endless reboots of *The Creature from the Black Lagoon*. ●

TV DINNERS

"Now he never touches fresh food at home except for an occasional salad. His dinner guests are taken into his freezer and allowed to pick out just what they feel they'd like; one may take egg foo-young, another oyster stew, another curried chicken, and so on. None of this nonsense of everybody at the table eating the same thing."

— FROZEN-FOOD PIONEER WILLIAM MAXSON, DESCRIBED IN A *NEW YORKER* PROFILE, 1945

TIME OF ORIGIN: *1953*

ORIGIN IN: *C. A. Swanson & Sons, Omaha*

HYPE FACTOR: *8 — In 1952, there was no market segment demanding flavorless, high-sodium frozen food. The success of the TV dinner rests entirely with sustained, well-funded, and well-executed hype.*

IMPACT FACTOR: *4 — Quality and variety have certainly improved over the years; meanwhile, home cooking has survived — and even thrived — in the age of frozen meals. Shall we call it a modest win for all sides?*

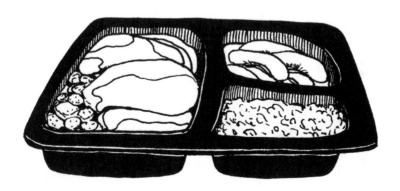

Today, the average American eats 72 frozen meals each year — that's one every five days. Sixty years ago, that number was zero. With up to 40 percent of us eating fast food every single day and fully half of our meals prepared outside the home, it's no surprise that the average family eats together fewer than five times every week.

Convenience food is an artifact of the twentieth century that has radically reshaped the way humankind eats. Where once the scarcity of food and the difficulty of its preparation led naturally to low-calorie diets and ritualized communal dining, packaged ready-to-eat food makes it easy to snack on our own, on the go — and without stopping, since convenience foods also give us megadoses of the energy-rich sugars and fats that half a million years of subsistence foraging has programmed our species to crave.

Left to police ourselves in the face of limitless temptation, we modern Americans have developed a uniquely self-tormenting relationship with food: We count calories, study food labels, and obsess about nutrition. With our food largely unmoored from tradition and even from nature, many eaters are looking to recapture a now-shattered stability — some fetishize honest farm food with an intensity that would have mystified our great-grandparents, while others turn to quasi-scientific diets and food systems that offer a pretense of lab-coated certainty and reassurance.

While we cannot blame all this on a single factor, there's no denying that the advent of frozen dinners was a decisive step in our disruption of traditional eating. By nudging eating America away from the dinner table and into the living room, Swanson's TV dinners helped set us on our present path of unmindful eating.

THE ARTIFICIAL-ICE AGE

Human beings have long recognized that low temperatures extend food life. For as long as we've had a nation, Americans have preserved food through refrigeration in naturally cool cellars that were sometimes kept even cooler with purchased ice, generally cut from frozen lakes. By the mid-nineteenth century, an interstate ice trade kept many cities supplied year-round with the essential material not just for preserving food but also for making the ice creams, slushes, and sorbets that were becoming favorite treats. But frozen food had severely limited commercial potential before the arrival of mechanical freezers late in the century.

While freezing is effective at arresting decay, it can also be quite destructive to the food it preserves. Through osmosis, ice can rob food of its flavor and nutrition, and jagged ice crystals can lacerate cell walls, yielding a soggy, unpalatable product when thawed. However, in the early 1920s, Clarence Birdseye perfected a flash-freezing technique that minimized cell damage. Now tender peas and delicate fish fillets could be frozen and still offer a taste and appearance that was better than anything from a can.

Insiders of the processed food industry, which had been steadily growing since the mid-nineteenth century, predicted that Birdseye's invention was going to be huge. So with the backing of General Foods, the Bird's Eye label started selling nationwide a range of frozen meats, vegetables, and fruits in the 1930s.

But sales were slow. Flash freezing was indeed a revolutionary technology — and it had outpaced consumers. Electric refrigerators were still relatively new. Many homes had little if any freezer space, and markets were disinclined to install expensive freezer units if no one was going to buy. Nevertheless, corporations in the early twentieth century still considered the long game so they didn't give up on frozen food. Eventually the market started catching up, and by 1941 Bird's Eye had sold 100 million pounds of frozen product.

THE WAR DIVIDEND

World War II was a blessing for American industry and for the processed-food industry in particular. Stimulated by the military's demand for portable, easy-to-prepare food with an indefinite shelf life, packagers stepped up production of canned food and innovated an arsenal of freeze-dried, condensed, and powdered foods. Back on the home front, shoppers were facing fewer choices on depleted grocery shelves and many started trying frozen food for the first time.

When peace returned, processors, determined to maintain wartime production levels, unleashed a bizarre menagerie of food products on an unsuspecting public. The hungry and adventurous could find everything from canned deep-fried hamburgers and canned bacon to powdered orange juice and frozen coffee concentrate; in addition to the still-familiar Spam, there were rival canned luncheon "meats" Treet, Mor, Prem, and Snack.

It is against this unsettling backdrop of supply-driven variety that frozen meals entered the marketplace. While many postwar food novelties quickly disappeared, frozen meals endured to become the emblem of the newly dawned era of convenience foods.

THE COLD WARS

It took a few attempts, however, before frozen meals gained a toehold in America's homes. The first contender was inventor William Maxson's self-named company, which got its start supplying frozen meals to naval aircraft during the war. First out of the gate, Maxson's Strato-Plates defined the frozen-meal paradigm: a meat entrée with two vegetable sides served in a three-compartment disposable tray.

After the war, Maxson's dinners were served to civilians on Pan American flights under the way-less-cool name Sky Plates. Plans to enter the retail market were warmly greeted by such outlets as the *New York Times*, the *New Yorker*, and *Better Food* magazine, but, for a number of reasons — including the death of the founder — Sky Plates never made the jump to the home kitchen.

In 1947, Frigi-Dinner of Philadelphia started distributing frozen dinners wholesale to airlines, railroads, and bars. To the usual selections of ham, meat loaf, beef stew, and veal cutlets, Frigi-Dinner inexplicably added chicken chow mein and egg rolls. However, it was the One-Eyed Eskimo brand, made by Frozen Dinner, Inc., that first tapped the home market. In 1950, the company sold more than 400,000 meals in the Pittsburgh area. In 1952, Frozen Dinner expanded and became the Quaker State Food Corp. Within two years, it had sold another two million dinners throughout the East Coast.

A GLACIAL CHANGE

Though an impressive figure on its own, two million frozen dinners in two years becomes staggeringly insignificant when you consider the nearly half a billion meals Americans ate *every day* in 1952.

While food writers and the food industry remained bullish on frozen foods, consumers were less welcoming. This was partially because many

Americans were still short on freezer space. But from the point of view of producers, a more intractable problem was that Americans were simply uninterested in the goods on offer.

That's the thesis of food writer Laura Shapiro, who, having sifted through the evidence, has revised the common assumption that postwar dinners eagerly embraced the glittering world of convenience and modernity offered by processed foods. To the contrary, she argues, after the food rationing of World War II, Americans wanted real home cooking, and women still overwhelmingly felt it was their duty to prepare it for their families from scratch.

The packaged food industry's chief boast — convenience — fell on many deaf ears: According to multiple polls in the late '40s and early '50s, cooking was by far women's favorite household chore. While it had been truly onerous in their grandmothers' time, modern conveniences such as gas or electric burners, accurately calibrated ovens, dishwashers, garbage disposals, and Tupperware considerably eased the burden. On average, women now spent less than two hours per day in the kitchen — almost an hour less than they had as recently as 1926.

To change America's opinion about convenience foods and reset its taste buds was going to require muscle. One of the companies that had that muscle was the Omaha-based C. A. Swanson & Sons, the nation's largest processor of turkeys.

PITCH-PERFECT

Swanson's frozen-meal business has a marvelous origin story. It stars 260 tons of unsold Thanksgiving turkeys, ten refrigerated railroad cars, and one brilliant and slightly unscrupulous salesman.

According to legend, Swanson had overestimated turkey sales for Thanksgiving 1953. Stuck with half a million pounds of frozen birds and nowhere to keep them, the company loaded them onto ten freezer train cars, which had to stay continually moving in order to keep the electricity flowing.

Meanwhile, halfway across the country, enterprising Swanson representative Gerry Thomas was in Pittsburgh having a look at the test kitchens of Frozen Dinners, Inc., an associated company that was supplying frozen meals for Pam Am Airlines. Spying a single-compartment aluminum food tray, he had an idea. Secreting a tray away in his jacket, Thomas tinkered with it on the flight back to Omaha until he had produced a three-compartment prototype — one for a turkey entrée with stuffing and gravy, and two smaller ones for sides of whipped sweet potatoes and peas. Back at corporate HQ, Thomas's pitch for a frozen turkey diner was warmly received by relieved Swanson executives.

That's the story that was promulgated by Thomas himself. Although it's been challenged by Swanson family members and at least one coworker, it's simply too good to die. Thomas, who himself died in 2005, was inducted into the Frozen Food Hall of Fame, and his handprints were immortalized on the Hollywood Walk of Fame.

The actual genesis of Swanson's frozen meals was almost certainly the much duller story of normal expansion into a new market. Since 1949, the company had been manufacturing heat-and-serve turkey potpies, which sold as briskly as 250,000 a day. Clearly, there was some demand for frozen meals, and it was time to jump into the market before it was saturated.

But that's not nearly as sexy a yarn as Thomas's one of unconsumed turkeys and flashes of insight in desperate moments. At the end of the day, it is the compelling narrative that won out. And that moral also encapsulates the success of Swanson's frozen TV dinner.

WHAT'S IN A NAME?

Experts agree it was brilliant marketing that made Swanson's frozen meals a success. After all, the technology was old, the product already familiar, and Swanson's tasted no better than the competition.

The first smart move was to reverse the One-Eyed Eskimo strategy and avoid referencing freezing in the name — because, to consumers, that was just a liability. Instead, Swanson went high-tech, as Maxson had done with the Strato-Plates, but brought it closer to home: Behold the TV dinner!

In the early 1950s, televisions were the hottest consumer technology. In just eight years, TV ownership had gone from less than 1 percent to 50 percent of all households — a faster proliferation than either the telephone or indoor plumbing had enjoyed. By calling its frozen meal the *TV dinner*,

Swanson hitched its product to a cultural phenomenon. It would be like launching an iDinner in 2007.

Swanson used all its weight to ensure its new product would break through, launching a national advertising campaign it called "Operation Smash." Even the packaging was a bold and dizzyingly meta-statement, depicting in glorious six-color printing a wood-grained console TV set with the meal itself, heated and ready for eating, on the screen. A USDA inspection stamp in one corner and price label in the other were disguised as tuner and volume dials, while the ingredients list was boxed at the bottom like a TV speaker.

The TV theme was more than a gimmick — it was a mission statement. Wordlessly but effectively, it redefined the purpose of frozen meals. Sure, they were convenient, but their goal wasn't to enable the sheer laziness: It was to bring families together — around the miracle of television.

The TV dinner debuted in 1954, and Swanson quickly cornered the frozen dinner market, selling some 13 million meals each year. Swanson dropped the name "TV dinner" in 1962, but the name stuck with consumers. Just as "facial tissue" was "Kleenex" and "photocopies" would be "Xeroxes," for years to come any "frozen meal" was a "TV dinner."

A BIG CHILL?

Within two years of the TV dinner's launch, 25 competitors were offering their own alternatives, and the frozen-food industry as a whole had become a $1.5 billion business. And for 50 years it continued to grow.

But tastes change. Frozen food peaked in 2008 and frozen meals actually declined 3 percent between 2009 and 2013. Industry watchers explain that foodie consciousness has been spreading. Now more people enjoy cooking fresh food and see it as a healthier choice. Forty percent of US adults believe that frozen dinners have no nutritional value. Demographics play a considerable role as well: More than half the people buying frozen food are over 44.

But theses reversals in frozen food are in the context of a tremendous market. Frozen meals are still a $9 billion industry, and more than 99 percent of households have frozen foods — that's just slightly less than the percentage of households that include one or more people who breathe oxygen.

The TV dinner itself is long gone, but the activity it inspired is still very much a part of American life: Sixty-six percent of us are still eating dinner in front of the television. ●

THE PILL

"You wined me and dined me
When I was your girl.
Promised if I'd be your wife
You'd show me the world.
But all I've seen of this old world
Is a bed and a doctor bill.
I'm tearin' down your brooder house
'Cause now I've got the pill!"

— LORETTA LYNN, FROM "THE PILL," 1975

TIME OF ORIGIN: *1960*

ORIGIN IN: *Worcester, Massachusetts*

HYPE FACTOR: *9 — Sex! Sometimes women like to have it!*

IMPACT FACTOR: *9 — Knowing you won't get pregnant won't solve all your problems as a woman. But it's a pretty awesome thing not to have to worry about.*

An inexpensive, reasonably safe, and extremely effective form of birth control that's as convenient as taking an aspirin: If we didn't already have the combined oral contraception pill — otherwise known simply as *the pill* — we might think it as fantastically utopian as that unrealized — and unrealizable — staple of science fiction, the food pill. [See **Synthetic Food**]

When the FDA approved the sale of the birth control pill in May 1960, it really felt as though history had made a quantum leap into the future. Chemistry had at last found a means of liberating humankind from our biological destiny, of severing sexuality from reproduction. But the seismic impact of the pill was felt most acutely as a cultural, not a scientific, phenomenon.

When the pill was approved, contraception was illegal in 30 states and restricted by federal law. The Catholic Church formally condemned it, and decent people wouldn't talk about it. Many Americans were deeply disturbed by this hubristic manipulation of nature and predicted sexual anarchy and the breakdown of the family. Countless more, however, saw it as a salvation. Arguably the most significant invention of the twentieth century, the contraceptive pill allowed women to take control of their bodies as never before in human history, to better manage their careers and plan their families, and to enjoy sexuality in a way that previously had been available only to men.

A NATURAL IMBALANCE

The 1975 single "The Pill," which generated controversy for country-music star Loretta Lynn as it worked its way up the charts, is a satirical take on the sexual politics of contraception. The song is about a wife who has been tethered to the home through a series of unwanted pregnancies. Resentful, she feels like a hen consigned to an egg farm, while her cock-of-the-walk husband carouses at bars with chicks who are more game to him than his harried housewife. But then the pill gives this mother hen control of her body and her freedom. Maternity gowns now exchanged for miniskirts and hot pants, this newly liberated chick is ready to hit the honky-tonks just like her philandering husband, and now she's laying down the law.

The song ends with an unexpected reconciliation. Freed from her role as mother and living life with gusto again, the singer rekindles passion with her husband. Both sides can now enjoy the intimacies of married life without just one of them left to bear the responsibility of the consequences. By giving her control of her sexuality, the pill has made the wife a true partner in her marriage.

Lynn's musical vignette is exactly the happy ending that women's rights activists envisioned when they began the birth control movement almost a century earlier.

Through the nineteenth century, human activity was perceived as taking place within two complementary but increasingly segregated spheres: the private life of the home and the public life of work. Men — strong and aggressive by nature — were suited for the cut and thrust of public life,

where fortunes were won and the fragile boundaries of the home defended. Women, on the other hand, were the agents of civilization. Fashioned by nature to be mothers, they were meant to nurture, to soften the brutish edges of the male sex, and to instill gentility and godliness in the home.

Theoretically, the roles assigned to the sexes were equally necessary, but as we know from history, separate but equal rarely is. Too often for women, the social bargain meant a lifetime of boredom or drudgery, with little need for education and few options beyond mothering and keeping house.

To turn-of-the-century feminists, then, breaking the link between womanhood and motherhood represented the fundamental step in liberating women and elevating their status. Once women could control their fertility, they would have the freedom to enter public life. Once there, they could stand or fall on their individual merits, just as men did.

THE MOTHER OF BIRTH CONTROL

This line of argument was not just theoretical to the chief driving force behind the pill, women's rights activist Margaret Sanger. She had seen the heavy toll pregnancy exacted on women, both socially and physically. Her own mother had given birth 11 times, miscarried seven, and died utterly spent in 1898 at the age of 50. As a visiting nurse in the slums of Manhattan's Lower East Side, Sanger saw this story repeated every day. Since federal and state laws prohibited contraception, she also witnessed the desperate extremes women would go to avoid another unwanted pregnancy: It was too often her job to minister to women suffering from the sometimes fatal complications of illegal abortions or from the dubiously sourced and euphemistically labeled "feminine hygiene" concoctions that could be obtained semi-legally from drugstores and whose prominently labeled "side effects" included miscarriage.

Sanger devoted herself to spearheading civil disobedience campaigns against what she called "stupid laws" restricting contraception. In fact, it was Sanger who coined the disarmingly frank (for the time) expression *birth control*. She began by writing a weekly family-planning newspaper column, which grew into a newsletter. That, in turn, led to Sanger's opening a women's health clinic in Brooklyn in 1914, the direct ancestor of Planned Parenthood.

Sanger was arrested and tried several times, but she also garnered support for her cause and had an effect on the law. A New York appeals court judge was persuaded that disease prevention served a legitimate public good, and so the ban was removed from condoms — although only as prophylactics (that is to say *disease preventers*) and not as contraceptives (i.e., baby preventers). Since condoms are both simultaneously, the decision was a victory for family-planning advocates, in substance if not in law.

THE MAGIC PILL

Condoms were not an insignificant victory. But Sanger wanted a device that would put fertility decisions entirely in women's hands. Having compiled a wish list of features for her ideal woman-centered contraceptive, she sought out individuals with the medical skill to produce it — and she was roundly disappointed. Pharmaceutical companies and research scientists, intimidated by the legal restrictions and social taboos around contraception, had no interest in developing Sanger's magic pill.

At a Manhattan diner party in 1950, she finally met someone who didn't say no. Instead, he asked how much money she had for her idea.

That man was Dr. Gregory Pincus. As a Harvard researcher in the 1930s, Pincus had been an enfant terrible. Imperious, outspoken, and an enthusiastic technologist, he was a world leader in hormone research who also kept a higher profile than Harvard thought was becoming for a serious scholar. The publicity became even worse when Pincus generated the world's first in vitro rabbit — or "fatherless" rabbit, as the newspapers called it. They also called *him* Harvard's Frankenstein and compared his

COMSTOCK LAWS

From the late nineteenth century to the early 1970s, America's sexual mores were enforced through a series of laws advocated by and named after social reformer Anthony Comstock, a zealous member of the YMCA and founder of the New York Society for the Suppression of Vice.

Comstock had been converted to his crusade by witnessing the depravity of post–Civil War New York City. As the nation industrialized, the population was moving away from farms and into the cities, where enterprising young men found opportunity aplenty — for work as well as for recreation of the most salacious kind. There was drinking, gambling, and, in Comstock's estimation, a hair-raising amount of sexual activity.

Although Comstock was deeply devout, his objection to sexuality was not entirely moral. Like many of his era, he believed that excessive lust drained a person's animal spirits, leaving him (it's almost always a *him* that's being considered) feeble, prone to mental and physical illness, and unsuitable for work. Pleasure and business did not mix.

Following intense lobbying by Comstock and a coalition of other business and religious leaders, Congress passed a law in 1873 that prohibited the sending of obscene material through the mail. The definition of obscenity covered not only prophylactic and contraceptive devices but even *information* about contraception. The states soon followed in crafting mini-Comstock statutes of their own.

work to the laboratory-incubated humans predicted in Aldous Huxley's then-new dystopian novel *Brave New World*. Pincus accepted his notoriety in good sport, but Harvard did not. In 1936, the university denied him tenure — which is the polite, collegial way of firing a professor.

Now a rogue academic, Pincus set up as an independent researcher and was always on the lookout for a cash infusion to keep his operation viable.

For Sanger, Pincus was a godsend. He may not have been a movement feminist, but he did share her ardent belief in population control, and, also like her, regarded sex as a source of pleasure rather than shame. He had shown himself an independent and dogged scientist, unafraid of defying

In the topsy-turvy moral universe of the Comstock laws, sex itself was the enemy, and the social ills and personal tragedy of unwanted pregnancy and sexually transmitted disease (which had been spreading at an alarming rate since the Civil War) were useful allies: If individuals lacked the inherent willpower to abstain, fear of the consequences might help keep them in line. After all, the wages of sin were nature's own correctives.

Thus anti-vice movement and the birth control activists found themselves precisely misaligned. In the Comstock status quo, marriage was regarded as the institution that defended society against unbridled sexuality. It constrained men's lust and protected women by ensuring that their children had legally accountable fathers. By weakening the link between sex and procreation, contraception was perceived as an assault on marriage itself that gave both parties less reason to enter into it in the first place, thus undermining an institution that promoted social stability and productivity.

Like Prohibition in the 1920s, the Comstock laws were selectively enforced and mostly intended to police marginal populations. As sexual mores loosened, the laws were less and less frequently observed. Nevertheless, when the pill was released in 1960, a majority of states still restricted or entirely prohibited birth control. It wasn't until the 1965 case *Griswold v. Connecticut* that the Supreme Court ruled that married couples could not be denied contraceptives. In 1972, the court lifted the ban for the rest of us, and the Comstock laws were at last overturned.

authority or offending public sensibilities. Above all, though, he needed the opportunity Sanger offered — not just for the money but for a last shot at reestablishing his reputation as a preeminent biochemist.

OUTLAW SCIENCE

Sanger used money from Planned Parenthood to set Pincus up with a meager lab. But the pill might never have been realized if Sanger hadn't found an unexpected patron. Katharine McCormick was an ally from the suffrage days. Since then, however, she had retired to care for her deeply schizophrenic husband. When he died, he left behind a vast fortune, and

Katharine, now in her 70s, resolved to do something monumental with it. She reconnected with Sanger, who pitched the pill.

McCormick, who was one of the first women to earn a degree from MIT, flew out to Boston to interview Pincus herself. After an extensive grilling, she gave him $40,000 on the spot and pledged her full support. She also stayed in Boston, to keep an eye on his progress.

Because Massachusetts had a total ban on contraception, Pincus had to be evasive, even downright deceptive, about the purpose of his research. During clinical testing, the pill was presented as a fertility drug. In 1957, it was presented to the FDA for approval as a treatment for "menstrual disorders."

Overnight, tens of thousands of American woman realized that they suffered from disordered menstruation.

A BELATED SEXUAL REVOLUTION

In 1960, all pretense was finally dropped, and the pill was approved as a birth control device.

A jubilant Katharine McCormick went to her doctor and demanded a prescription. Now in her 80s, she was indulging in a purely symbolic gesture, but she too wanted to exercise a freedom that she had fought for so long to provide all women.

Not everyone was so enthusiastic. A 1966 cover story in *U.S. News and World Report* speculated whether the pill might lead to "sexual anarchy." In support, it breathlessly cited a California "wife-swapping" scandal and reports of Long Island housewives turning to prostitution for fun and profit — sometimes behind their husbands' backs.

But critics who blamed the pill for the sexual revolution of the Swinging '60s had the causality backward. As revolutionary as it was, the birth control pill itself was a symptom of attitudes toward sex that had been liberalizing well before the Summer of Love. The 1953 Kinsey Report and the later research of Masters and Johnson famously revealed that American's sexual practices diverged dramatically from their public avowals. Half of all women had engaged in pre-marital sex, and one in four had cheated on her spouse.

Tens of thousands of couples were already using contraception, despite legal and religious prohibitions, and tens of thousands more were looking for an alternative as simple and effective as the pill. If the 1950s had actually been as repressed as it is sometimes caricatured, then even Sanger's will and McCormick's fortune would have foundered against the bastion of the law and public opinion.

A 1967 *Time* magazine cover story marks the end of the initial birth control pill panic. Did the pill promote promiscuity? Probably. But no more than the car or the drive-in movie theater had.

Family life and civilization would survive. ●

SYNTHETIC FOOD

"The general [foodie] ethos of natural, fresh, organic, bright — this is the opposite."

— ROBERT RHINEHART, CREATOR OF LIQUID MEAL REPLACEMENT SOYLENT

TIME OF ORIGIN: *1962*

ORIGIN IN: Friendship 7 *capsule, low Earth orbit*

HYPE FACTOR: 5 — *While synthetic food was ubiquitous in science fiction, the idea never had deep appeal in real life.*

IMPACT FACTOR: *1 — With today's options for convenient eating, only the truly committed techno-utopian geek can get behind the idea of complete liberation from the food chain.*

On February 20, 1962, the spacecraft *Friendship 7*, carrying astronaut John Glenn, lifted off from Cape Canaveral, Florida. This Mercury 6 mission made Glenn the third American to enter space and the first to orbit the Earth.

Glenn also has the distinction of being the first American to eat in space. His astro-meal consisted of applesauce squeezed from an aluminum tube, which he washed down with an orange-flavored powdered drink mix called Tang. Hardly anyone remembers the applesauce, but the drink was history-making.

Tang became an emblem of the space age. With a list of ingredients that includes lots of things you'd find in a chemistry lab and less than 2 percent "natural flavor," the powdered drink mix also became a bellwether for the breaching of another frontier: the brave new world of synthetic food.

SPACE-AGE FOOD FOR SPACE-AGE FOLK

Tang was developed in the late 1950s by food scientist William A. Mitchell. It is rumored to have been intended as a more nutritious competitor to Kool-Aid — which, if true, was a remarkably low bar to set for the chemical genius who would also give the world Cool Whip and Pop Rocks. To Kool-Aid's kid-pleasing formula of masses of sugar, boldly unnatural coloring, and nothing much else, Mitchell added an extra-large dose of vitamins C and A, a pinch more citric acid and a soupçon of natural flavors for a taste and tingly mouth feel not entirely un-evocative of orange juice.

Mitchell's laboratory drink was a flop: For moms, Tang was neither orangey nor convenient enough to displace frozen OJ from America's breakfast tables, while kiddies found it too juice-like to be fun.

Countless bottles of this pulpless imitation orange juice were languishing on supermarket shelves when Tang's unexpected cameo 162 miles above Earth catapulted it to stardom. Thanks to its continued presence on NASA's subsequent Gemini missions, Tang became inextricably identified with the space program. In fact, many consumers believed that it had been developed by NASA itself, an urban legend that General Foods, the actual manufacturer, did nothing to dispel.

Having embraced Tang, the American shopper started taking a second look at other powdered foods. Nondairy creamer, instant coffee and mashed potatoes, and dehydrated soups and sauces had been available at least since World War II; some products, like powdered milk, went way back to the nineteenth century. But these powders were by far the least popular of processed foods — which is no surprise, because they are, frankly speaking, gross. Now, with a chromium veneer of space-age glamour, they seemed exciting, modern, as finely engineered as an Atlas rocket to be superior to anything found in nature.

That gritty mouthfeel and bitter-tinny aftertaste was the flavor of progress.

SHAKING OFF THE SHACKLES OF NATURE

While gourmets of any era might consider industrialized food a crime against eating, the original proponents of ultra-processing imagined something far more noble than the burnt-tasting coffee crystals and starchy packets of instant béchamel that the food industry eventually provided.

For the vast majority of human existence, food insecurity was the norm. In even the wealthiest of societies, famine was just one sustained drought, one extended winter, one invading army away. The promise of food untethered to the whims of nature, food that could be made by human ingenuity to be abundant, portable, preservable, and cheap was a utopian dream with revolutionary potential. By meeting our basic biological needs, synthetic food — say, in the form of a pill — would allow us all to live with the freedom and security once reserved for the aristocracy. There would be no more leverage to force anyone into accepting dangerous or degrading jobs, fewer onerous domestic duties confining women to the home. Instead, each of us would be able to pursue meaningful avocations, laboring now to satisfy the demands not of the body but of the soul.

In the late nineteenth century, simultaneous developments in chemistry, industry, and politics made that moment seem tantalizingly near.

THE PROGRESSIVE PROMISE OF THE FOOD PILL

Alongside robots and jet packs, food pills complete the holy trinity of futuristic kitsch. They run the fantasy-adventure gamut, from the classic sci-fi of Isaac Asimov and Ray Bradbury to the space-race camp of TV's *Lost in Space* and *The Jetsons* (whose breakfast pills include burnt toast). Even the technophobic fantasies of J.R.R. Tolkien include food pills, in the form of *lembas*, an elvish sort of super trail mix.

The apotheosis of processed food, the meal in a pill seems an idea native to the twentieth century, but its origins lie in the Victorian era.

One of the first to speculate in earnest about food pills was the feminist, lawyer, and populist firebrand Mary Elizabeth Lease, who, as part of the hype building up to the Chicago World's Fair of 1893, was asked by the Associated Press to forecast the world of 1993. Lease predicted a future where the minimization of household chores would raise the status of women. She imagined future diners consuming

> in condensed form the rich loam of the earth, the life force
> or germs now found in the heart of the corn, in the kernel of
> wheat, and in the luscious juice of the fruits. A small phial of
> this life from the fertile bosom of mother Earth will furnish

men with substance for days. And thus the problems of cooks and cooking will be solved.

One year later, the eminent French chemist Marcellin Berthelot made a similar prediction, in equally purple prose and at much greater length, in an interview called "Foods in the Year 2000," which could be considered a synthetic-food manifesto.

In Berthelot's vision, at the dawn of the second millennium, chemistry will have replaced the unreliable bounty of Lease's Mother Nature: "a great proportion of our staple foods, which we now obtain through natural growth, would be manufactured direct, through the advance of synthetic chemistry, from their constituent elements, carbon, hydrogen, oxygen, and nitrogen." And why should anyone mourn the death of natural foods? After all, the professor asks readers to acknowledge that "the beefsteak of to-day is not the most perfect… in either color or composition."

In contrast, culinary chemists of the future will manufacture nutritionally optimal steak from the atoms up. Of course, it might not look much like meat as we know it. Nevertheless, "chemically, digestively, and nutritively speaking," it will be "the same identical food." As a matter of fact, he adds, "its form will differ, because it will probably be a tablet."

However, Berthelot's tablet is somewhere between a food pill proper and a *Star Trek* replicator meal, because the final product will be "of any color and shape that is desired, and will, I think, entirely satisfy the epicurean senses of the future." Berthelot is one of the few theorists of the food pill who bothers to consider flavor and appearance and not just nutrition. For all his techno-utopianism, Berthelot was, after all, still French. There is room in his engineered future for artificial wine, liquor, and even tobacco — perhaps a sneak preview of today's vaporizers.

Not everyone was as pro-pill as Lease and Berthelot. In the 1887 satiric novel *The Republic of the Future*, author Anna Dodd envisions with horror the food pellets prescribed by state scientists and distributed from centralized larders directly to kitchen-free homes via hundreds of miles of pneumatic tube. Though the 2050 dining experience might not recall the opulence of Victorian banquets, its refined nature suits the residents of New York Socialist City. It is also more egalitarian, since domestic science will have eliminated the need for both servants and housewives: "When the last pie was made into the first pellet, woman's true freedom began." Dodd's reactionary sympathies, however, lay entirely with the pies and the men.

A FUNNY THING HAPPENED
ON THE WAY TO THE FUTURE

Food pills were heralded repeatedly and with certainty. So why don't we have them?

Because a meal in a pill is an impossibility.

From simply an energy standpoint, no single pill can deliver what we need. An average adult woman needs about 2,000 calories per day. (Men require a few hundred more.) Oils and fats are the most calorie-rich foods, but — whether you go au naturel, à la Lease, and choose lard or prefer a more factory-refined oil as Berthelot might — it would take more than a cup of either for you to hit your calorie quota.

If that weren't enough bulk to scuttle the idea of a super-concentrated food system, most of us need between 26 and 40 grams of fiber if we'd like to avoid constipation and colon cancer. So let's add, say, a quarter cup of your favorite roughage.

Nutrition might seem an easier fix, since vitamins are measured in milligrams. However, there is some evidence suggesting that vitamin pills are not as effective as the vitamins we extract from actual food. In other words, Berthelot's hypothesis may have been mistaken — carbon or hydrogen in one context may not be quite the same as carbon or hydrogen in another. And, even if they are, there's always the possibility that there are critical aspects of nutrition that we still do not understand, such as micronutrients and who knows what else.

More than nutritional impracticalities, though, it was culture that killed the dream of the food pill. By the early '70s, space-age modernism had lost its luster. Industrialism was now synonymous with pollution and wastefulness, and technological fixes seemed soulless and authoritarian.

In 1970, the foodie movement was born when Alice Waters opened the restaurant Chez Panisse in Berkeley, California, a center of the back-to-the-land ethos of the hippie counterculture. Her food mantra — local, fresh, and in season — marked a return to a romantic belief like Lease's that nature provides and that the best thing a cook can do is not get in the way of the ingredients.

The Victorians who had looked hopefully toward a day when no-prep, no-clean-up food pills would be consumed in kitchenless homes would have been shocked by our early twenty-first-century fetish for homemade pickles, urban beekeeping, and artisanal ketchup. And handlebar mustaches: They probably would have been puzzled as to why we're still doing that too.

The death knell of synthetic food was *Soylent Green*, a 1973 sci-fi film that depicts a dystopian future ravaged by global warming and overpopulation, where the velvet-clad haves eat steak and drink bourbon in rococo condos, while the masses of have-nots squat in tenements and subsist on a synthesized protein product… that turns out to be manufactured from — spoiler alert! — *human remains.*

Tang, Kool-Aid, Cool Whip, Nescafé, Cup-a-Soup, and the other mutant brainchildren of Professor Berthelot's synthetic food chemistry can still be found in any supermarket, but they are relics of a bygone era. Their moment of glory did not long outlive NASA's last visit to the moon, in 1972.

FOOD HACKING

But, like Frankenstein's monster, any idea as audacious as human-manufactured food cannot die forever.

Synthetic food might have lost its savor decades ago, but it has thrived in one form: liquid meal replacements. From Carnation Instant Breakfast, which debuted in 1964, to Slimfast, Ensure, and more, these nutritional supplements target consumers with specific concerns: bodybuilders who want to bulk up, the elderly too frail cook, dieters weaning themselves from the pleasures of mealtime.

Along with energy bars and a new generation of juice cleanses and diets, liquid meal replacements have nearly normalized the idea that nutrition and cuisine can be separated, that there is eating for survival and then there is recreational eating.

Among a new population disrupting the idea of eating is Robert Rhinehart. The electrical engineer turned entrepreneur/food scientist is pioneering a new return to the nineteenth-century techno-utopian dream of synthetic food.

Dismayed at the inconvenience of microwaving corn dogs and boiling instant ramen when he was living the start-up life in San Francisco's Tenderloin district, Rhinehart figured that there had to be an easier and cheaper way to keep his body alive enough to keep coding. So he started on a crash course in nutrition. Determining 35 essential nutrients, he blended them up and then began blogging about his experiences as he lived off his formula for a month. Rhinehart named his nutrition drink Soylent — thus proving yet again that, however much they might try, electrical engineers fundamentally do not understand irony.

On his blog, Rhinehart posted his motivating hypothesis: "The body doesn't need food itself, merely the chemicals and elements it contains.... Besides olive oil for fatty acids and table salt for sodium and chloride nothing [in my drink] is recognizable as food." This is a perfect paraphrase of the vision that Marcellin Berthelot was promulgating exactly 120 years earlier.

Like any Silicon Valley entrepreneur, Rhinehart is as much an evangelist as he is a businessman: He's not just marketing rebranded Ensure to time-strapped and taste-challenged techies: He's "hacking the body" and combating global hunger.

And it may not be all hype: At three calories a penny in Rhinehart's reckoning, or about $7 for a day's worth of nutrition, Soylent — if it ever sees full-scale production — would be no more expensive than fast food but vastly more healthful. And while the product still might be prohibitively expensive for people in developing nations, Rhinehart hopes one day to engineer genetically altered Soylent-producing algae, which would make the drink essentially free.

A secondary benefit of turning to a synthetic diet would be the scaling-back of industrial agriculture, which is currently straining the environment. For instance, livestock is responsible for almost 15 percent of greenhouse gases; and in drought-wracked California, agriculture consumes 80 percent of the state's water.

But even agricultural disruption was anticipated by Bertholot more than 100 years ago: "At some more or less distant period in the future, synthetic chemistry will destroy all the great agricultural industries, and put to new uses the grain fields and cattle ranges of to-day."

Let's give the father of synthetic chemistry the last word:

> If the surface of the earth ceases to be divided, and I may
> say disfigured, by the geometrical devices of agriculture, it
> will regain its natural verdure of woods and flowers.... The
> favored portions of the earth will become vast gardens, in
> which the human race will dwell amid a peace, a luxury, and
> an abundance recalling the Golden Age of legendary lore.

Someone should get this guy a TED Talk. •

EASY LISTENING

"Isn't the rattle of your neighbor's garbage can lids enough without having to listen to freaked-out music? Pull yourself out of your old radio routine and get into something nice and sweet."

— WDBM-FM RADIO PROMO

TIME OF ORIGIN: *Mid-1960s*

ORIGIN IN: *FM radio*

HYPE FACTOR: *2 — Aside from self-congratulatory radio promos bashing the kids and their crazy rock music, there wasn't much buzz about easy listening.*

IMPACT FACTOR: *2 — While easy listening had huge numbers initially, assimilation and the cold embrace of the grave eventually culled the herd.*

With the rise of rock 'n' roll, teenage taste dominated the singles music market. But on the home stereo, at the office, in the grocery store, and on elevators, the adults still called the musical shots. And what they demanded was easy listening, a simplified, soothing, and upbeat style of music that would eventually assume the role of the anti–rock 'n' roll and that would galvanize both sides of the generation gap in the 1960s and '70s.

MUZAK: THE COMPANY

Like the noun *Kleenex* and the verb *to google*, *Muzak* is a generic term that derives from a brand name. Although you don't hear the name invoked so often anymore, Muzak was a background music distribution services that was at one time infamous for piping insipid instrumental rerecordings of popular songs into public spaces. (The renamed company still does so today, except the music is no longer rerecorded, so Muzak is harder to spot.) Eventually, Muzak would inspire a radio format called "easy listening" or "beautiful music" that dominated FM stations and tormented generations of rock-hungry kids trapped in the family station wagon during errand runs and trips to grandma's house.

In origin, however, Muzak was not a style of music but rather a technology for delivering sound along telephone and power lines. The innovation was the brainchild of George Owen Squier, an army officer and inventor, who promoted the idea in the early twentieth century as an alternative to radio, which was then still an expensive and unreliable developing technology. In 1922, Squier licensed his invention to form Wired Radio. Hoping to steal a little marketing pizzazz from George Eastman's phenomenally successful Kodak photography empire, Wired Radio changed its name to Muzak (*mus*ic + Kod*ak*) in 1934.

By then radio was secure in the home marketplace, so Muzak pivoted to supply background music to businesses like hotels and restaurants. Skyscrapers, which were beginning to loom over the nation's largest cities, used the soft, reassuring sounds of Muzak to relieve the anxiety of jittery elevator passengers — and thus another pejorative entered the lexicon: *elevator music.*

MUZAK: THE CURSE

In the 1940s, Muzak focused on conquering America's office spaces. The cornerstone of its strategy was a trademarked concept called "Stimulus Progression." Based on a battery of pseudoscientific efficiency research, Stimulus Progression was a theory of song sequencing that purported to counterbalance the natural ebb and flow of the listener's energy. Programming was grouped into 15-minute blocks of music whose intensity gradually built, giving spirits a gentle lift, and, supposedly, increasing productivity when broadcast into the workplace.

Intensity is, of course, a relative term.

In its earliest days, Muzak played the same sort of music you would hear on the radio. Since sheet music sales ruled the day, popular songs were oftentimes performed by more or less anonymous orchestras. But as recording stars — singers with individual styles and lyrical phrasing — emerged, Muzak began to part ways with popular music.

To offer its brand of tranquilly congenial sounds that would offend no one and fit in with its Stimulus Progression format, Muzak recorded its own arrangements of hit songs. Lyrics were dropped for fear that they might distract the listener. Also verboten were too overtly jazzy or danceable songs and brash instruments like saxophones. Lush string arrangements punctuated with twinkling piano riffs ruled the sonic world of Muzak.

In a weird feedback loop, Muzak artists became famous in their own right, as office drones willingly brought workplace music into their homes. Lawrence Welk, Mantovani, and 101 Strings were a few of the acts that made the crossover from Muzak to the more anemic end of the pop music spectrum. If you've never heard of them, count yourself lucky.

Muzak, the brand name, was well down the path of becoming *Muzak*, the cultural scourge.

EASY LISTENING

It took the polarizing assault of rock 'n' roll, however, for Muzak to emerge as a self-conscious cultural force.

In 1961, responding to pressure from radio stations that saw themselves as pop but nevertheless resisted rock 'n' roll, *Billboard* magazine created the easy-listening chart. (After several name changes, it's still with us as the adult contemporary singles chart.) For the first years, softer rock songs could cross over to easy listening, as Elvis's 1962 hit "Can't Help Falling in Love" did. In 1965, however, there was no overlap between the pop and easy-listening charts.

The charts indicated a growing gap in tastes between old and young. As the '60s progressed and rock music became increasingly identified with the counterculture of hippies who flouted social norms, questioned the tenets of capitalism, and vocally opposed the ongoing war in Vietnam, adults, in reaction, embraced with even greater ardor the most un-rock-like elements of their own music. They flocked to easy-listening radio stations, whose programming systematically erased all traces of what had been unbridled and provocative in the music of the not-so-distant past. Listeners would find no blaring brass of the boogie-woogie bands and none of Benny Goodman's screaming clarinet that heralded the swing era of the late 1930s.

There was no hint of the jitterbugs and bobby-soxers of the Second World War era. Even Frank Sinatra — paragon of Establishment-approved pop — could occasionally be too heavy for easy-listening stations.

But the cultural bulwark of easy listening could not completely beat back the changing times. Although they were reviled by America's grownups when their music first reached our shores, the Beatles were eventually accorded respect as songwriters. The first Beatles song to hit number one on the easy-listening chart was the 1968 Sérgio Mendes and Brasil '66 cover of "Fool on the Hill." By the early '70s, suitably denatured cover versions of "Eleanor Rigby," "Yesterday," and the George Harrison ballad "Something" (often mistakenly, if understandably, attributed to Paul McCartney) had become staples of beautiful-music stations, as had a number of songs from younger artists who, like Simon & Garfunkel, Chicago, and Blood, Sweat & Tears, strayed farther from rock.

San Francisco's KABL, which debuted in 1959 as one of the first easy-listening stations, had a typical programming system that closely resembled the Muzak model. The station classified its songs into four categories: full instrumentals, small instrumentals, vocals, and up-tempos. It would play one song from each category, in order, and then repeat these 15-minute programming blocks over and over again, switching songs but keeping the pattern.

A MUSIAL COUNTERREVOLUTION

Billboard's definition of *easy listening* was hazy. Pretty much anything not rock counted — although country and jazz were also excluded. But as the concept spread, easy listening sometimes became quite meticulously regulated under the rubric of beautiful music.

Like Muzak, much beautiful-music programming purported to be determined by focus groups and market research. Its target audience — 18- to 49-year-old women — included the quintessential housewife and mother whose nerves were forever at the fraying point. The last thing she wanted was for her music to reflect back the world around her, a world of race riots and political assassinations, of the mounting specter of crime and the drug culture, and of baffling and heartbreaking disrespect from her teenage kids. Like Muzak, too, easy listening was *instrumental* music — not

AN EASY GUIDE TO EASY LISTENING

THE CLASSICS
Pianos, strings, harpsichords, breathy choruses — and no trace of rock 'n' roll.
   - The Ray Conniff Singers, "Somewhere My Love," 1966
   - Percy Faith, "Theme from *A Summer Place*," 1960
   - Ferrante and Teicher, *Golden Themes from Motion Pictures*, 1962
   - Francis Lai, *A Man and a Woman* soundtrack, 1966
   - Paul Mauriat, "Love Is Blue," 1968

EASY LISTENING MUSIC BY POPULAR VOCALISTS
Occasionally bizarre but not uninteresting attempts to bridge the generation gap.
   - Frank Sinatra, *Strangers in the Night*, 1966
   - Barbra Streisand, *The Way We Were*, 1974
   - Andy Williams, *Alone Again (Naturally)*, 1972

EASY-LISTENING POP
   - Bread, *Baby I'm-a Want You*, 1972
   - The Carpenters, *Carpenters*, 1972
   - Neil Diamond, *Moods*, 1972
   - The 5th Dimension, *Greatest Hits on Earth*, 1972

just in the sense that it favored lyric-free songs, but also inasmuch as it was music whose sole purpose was pragmatic rather than aesthetic. The easy-listening housewife did not want to be challenged — she didn't even want to be entertained: She wanted to be sedated.

The appeal went far beyond women ages 18 to 49. Hand in hand, Muzak and beautiful music went on to dominate both the workplace and FM radio from the mid-'60s to the mid-'70s.

Enjoying bipartisan Establishment support, Muzak echoed throughout President Lyndon Johnson's Texas ranch and was also played at Richard Nixon's inauguration. Sailors on nuclear-armed Polaris submarines chilled out to Muzak. Heroes Buzz Aldrin and Neil Armstrong even listened to it during their moon shot.

When FM radio expanded in the mid-'60s, easy listening was waiting to fill the new bandwidth. In some idealistic pockets, however, freestyle radio developed, where DJs played obscure music for niche audiences of music adventurers and connoisseurs. Not surprisingly, many of these experimenters couldn't afford to keep the discs spinning and eventually succumbed to the disciplined and market-focused beautiful-music format.

As late as 1979, *Billboard* magazine called beautiful-music programming the number one radio format in the US. But it didn't last.

In the '80s and '90s, string arrangements and overorchestrated Beatles' covers seemed corny even to the ever-decreasing ranks of stay-at-home moms. As the virulently anti-rock demographic aged, their economic power dwindled and they became irrelevant to advertisers. Beautiful-music programming began to die.

Meanwhile, rock and rock-influenced pop had been around long enough to produce plenty of light ballads to sustain soft-rock radio, which challenged beautiful music for the frayed-nerve demographic. Besides, what was anyone resisting anymore? Rock had long since lost its bad-boy image. It was now hip-hop and gangster rap that were giving parents nightmares.

By the late '90s, even the venerable Muzak was forced to adapt or die. Now instead of seeking to create an entirely parallel style music though strategic adaptations of Top 40 hits, it plays originals like everyone else does. The Muzak magic now lies in the special selecting and mixing of songs to scientifically appeal to specific demographics.

Easy listening endures as a concept. But it has long since made its peace with rock. •

THE MIDLIFE CRISIS

"I don't think that I can take it,
'Cause it took so long to bake it,
And I'll never have that recipe again,
Oh, no!"

— RICHARD HARRIS, FROM THE 1968 HIT
SONG AND INCOMPREHENSIBLE ODE TO
MIDDLE-AGE ANGST, "MACARTHUR PARK"

TIME OF ORIGIN: *Mid-'60s to early '70s*

ORIGIN IN: *Pop psychology*

HYPE FACTOR: *9 — From self-pity to horror to unmitigated glee, there was a reason for everyone to watch the resulting cultural train wreck as adults for the first time attempted to accommodate themselves with the trappings and temptations of a triumphant youth culture.*

IMPACT FACTOR: *4 — Although it's still a useful term to employ whenever your "cool dad" embarrasses you with his potbelly and fluorescent skinny chinos, no one believes in it as a clinical label anymore.*

Since the teenager was invented 75 years ago, the cultural gap between youth and adulthood — or at least middle age — has never been narrower than it is today. From the '50s to the '90s, the transition into adulthood could be distilled into the act of "cutting your hair and putting on a tie." But changing workplace culture and broader social attitudes have made it easier for 30- and 40-somethings to hold on to the signifiers of their youth. Our current crop of established adults feel less pressure to take out that nose ring or cover up the tattoo they got back in college. They even find it charming to dress their toddlers in tiny versions of Blondie or Joy Division T-shirts, just like the tattered ones that still hang in their closets.

Thirty years ago, however, it was a different story. Such preoccupation with youth among entry-level oldsters was considered a psychological affliction. And it had a name: the midlife crisis.

YOUTH TRIUMPHANT

In the 1950s, adults regarded youth culture as something either to be ignored as trash or to be squelched as a source of juvenile delinquency. But by the mid-'60s, the "youthquake" had become an unstoppable cultural juggernaut that was setting trends for adults. On the cover of *Vogue*, waiflike models such as Twiggy, Jean Shrimpton, and Edie Sedgwick touted the miniskirt; and even in the staid world of men's fashion, the psychedelic ripples emanating from the boutiques of London's trendy Carnaby Street opened the monochromatic palette of the Man in the Gray Flannel Suit to a flash of color. Pants began to flare and sideburns to shadowed the cheeks of many a Madison Avenue exec.

As the hippies rallied around their exclusionary slogan "It's all over over 30," proclaiming their loyalty to the principles of free love, drug experimentation, and liberation from societal expectations, growing numbers of spectators on the wrong side of the age divide eyed the spectacle with grudging envy, wondering whether just perhaps they might be missing out on something.

A NEW MALADY FOR A NEW AGE

Although it was coined 11 years earlier, the term *midlife crisis* was popularized by the 1976 pop-psychology book *Passages*. While more tuned-in publications like *New York* magazine had been reporting on the phenomenon since 1972, it took time for the discontentment and self-questioning raised by the '60s to permeate every corner of the nation. But by mid-decade, awareness of the midlife crisis had peaked, and *Passages* rode the trend to become a publishing sensation.

Simplifying the conclusions of a number of psychological studies, which she augmented with her own interviews, author Gail Sheehy argued that personality is not fixed from childhood but changes as we face the challenges presented by various phases of life. According to Sheehy, the challenge of the late 30s and early 40s is coming to terms with life's limitations. After a

CULTURAL MONUMENTS TO THE MIDLIFE CRISIS

Although the term *midlife crisis* didn't catch on until the mid-'70s, the phenomenon itself was well documented earlier. Here are some definitive representations of the midlife crisis.

Seconds, John Frankenheimer, 1966

In this sci-fi-tinged and darkly comedic drama, a business- and family man (Rock Hudson) disenchanted with his life gets a second shot at it, thanks to the services of a mysterious company that disencumbers him from his past and gives him a new face and a new identity. Needless to say, it all goes terribly wrong.

I Love You, Alice B. Toklas, Hy Averback, 1968

The untimely appearance of a free-spirited hippie chick and a plate of psychedelic brownies derails the impending wedding of a 30-something attorney (Peter Sellers), catapulting the painfully unhip lawyer into the heart of L.A.'s flower power scene.

A Tramp Shining, Richard Harris, 1968

Billboard's number-two album of 1968 is a midlife crisis in sonic form, where lush easy-listening string arrangements collide with harpsichord flourishes, tambourines, and go-go brass that evoke the orchestrated pop sounds of late Beach Boys and the 5th Dimension. Consisting of tracks with titles like "Name of my Sorrow," "If You Must Leave my Life," and "In the Final Hours," actor Richard Harris' debut musical album (with songs by singer-songwriter Jim Webb) delivers four vinyl sides of regret, reproach,

lifetime of planning and struggle, one is finally at the peak — but the view from the top is of nothing but decline. Career, family, possessions, what does it all mean? Now that death and decay are on the horizon, what should be done with the time remaining? Accept our self-forged shackles and go quietly into the night, or burst out and grab at life one last time before strength entirely fades? Red sports car or torrid affair…?

and delicious, delicious self-pity. In a voice both honeyed and hoarse, Harris sings the reminiscences of a man clearly on the brink of middle age, brooding over squandered opportunities and pining for a redemptive love he knows may never come — and certainly would not last anyway.

The Hospital, Arthur Hiller, 1971
Bond girl Diana Rigg plays hippie-muse to George C. Scott's disillusioned hospital chief in this social satire with a murder-mystery twist. Writer Paddy Chayefsky (also known for the classic satire *Network*) won an Academy Award for his screenplay.

The Fall and Rise of Reginald Perrin, 1976–1979
Maddened by the monotony of his life, the titular hero of this BBC comedy series fakes his own death only to rise again by employing an absurdist business strategy predicated on selling obvious junk and making the worst decisions possible. Guess what happens next.

10, Blake Edwards, 1979
This film made British comedian Dudley Moore into a superstar, made cornrows an acceptable hairstyle for white women, made an estimated million dollars in royalties for *Boléro* (a classical composition from 1928), and made *midlife crisis* even more of a household phrase than it already was, generating a spate of similarly themed Blake Edwards sex farces. That's like a royal flush of early '80s trends. The premise of *10* is exactly the same as everything else on this list, but this time the hero is a successful composer and the milieu is the Beverly Hills jet set.

AN EPHEMERAL UNIVERSAL
The midlife crisis was hot, hot, hot for a decade or so. It provided fodder for news magazines, movies, and at least one plot thread for every single episode of the popular TV shows *The Love Boat* and *Fantasy Island*. And it did seem to identify a constant in human psychology. Considerable numbers of the Second World War generation were indeed in crisis as they

AN EQUAL-OPPORTUNITY DISORDER

With its emphasis on career dissatisfaction and declining virility, the midlife crisis was originally perceived as a man's problem. In fact, the earliest news stories refer to it as "the male midlife crisis." But there were tens of thousands of women in crisis too. In the wake of the women's liberation movement, a generation of housewives wanted to know what they had sacrificed by following the script and opting for marriage and family.

Premiering in 1970, the situation comedy *The Mary Tyler Moore Show* presented the story of a single woman in her early 30s moving to the city to start a career and begin a new life on her own. It spoke equally to questioning mothers and their hopeful daughters. Reflecting the uncertainty of the era, the original theme song opened with the question, "How will you make it on your own?" For season two, however, the lyric was changed to end with an emphatic "You're gonna make it after all!"

confronted the social changes of the '60s and '70s with an unstable mix of disgust and desire. And their baby-boomer children were confronting crisis too. As the idealism of the '60s curdled, many hippies jumped from one extreme to another and, in their new guise as yuppies, started to pursue wealth, status, and *stuff* with more ardor than their parents ever had. What else but midlife crisis could explain that?

The midlife crisis was real enough, but it was roots were more cultural than psychological. The progression outlined in *Passages* was a particular middle-class phenomenon that assumed a specific timeline of college, career, and marriage, which has become more fluid over time. Bearing the brunt of families wrecked by midlife crises, Gen Xers coming of age in the '80s and '90s took a more skeptical view of careers and were in no hurry to get married: On both counts, they wanted to be certain before they committed. Taking life at their own pace, Xers have experienced the traumas of aging over a longer time, which has made a crisis-inducing cluster more of a rarity.

To suit the new reality, the midlife crisis has been redefined so broadly that it is nearly meaningless. It can happen anywhere between the ages of 40 and 60; it can be triggered by dissatisfaction with the career you have or your regret at never obtaining one; you might be mourning your empty nest or your decision not to have children, or the fact that you married too early or still haven't married. Maybe a parent's passing or your own health issues have made you uncomfortably aware of the reality of death.

Bored by your routine? Tired of your friends or your spouse? Of yourself? Are you drinking more? Less? Do you fantasize about having an affair — or maybe you've lost interest in sex entirely? Have you lost your motivation? Or perhaps you're experiencing a sudden surge of energy and ambition? You may be having a midlife crisis.

Even with such sweeping criteria, though, only 10 to 26 percent of adults over 40 report having experienced a midlife crisis. •

IRONY

"There was the sense that everything is rubbish and all rubbish is wonderful."

— DAVID BOWIE IN 2002, RECALLING 1972

"Fall falling, falling and laughing, falling and laughing, falling and laughing."

— SCOTTISH NEW WAVE BAND ORANGE JUICE,
FROM THEIR SONG "FALLING AND LAUGHING," 1982

TIME OF ORIGIN: *July 6, 1972*

ORIGIN IN: *BBC TV's* Top of the Pops

HYPE FACTOR: *6 — While the volume never gets turned up too high, media storms over irony, its imminent demise, and its unavoidable return, blow by every few years.*

IMPACT FACTOR: *7 — While irony hasn't been exactly paradigm-shifting, it has conditioned the way we experience and express our pleasures. It may have made us more acutely aware of the gap between ourselves and our conception of ourselves, and it's also presented a difficult obstacle for successive generations of pop culture to clear.*

Snark. Hate-watching bad TV. Consciously wearing passé fashions as a joke, or as a nostalgic embrace of the glamour and style so lacking in contemporary life. The dreaded "air quotes." These are but a few examples of the way irony has insinuated itself into our lives.

Irony exists in the gap between what is said and what is actually meant. It assumes a psychological attitude that is comfortable with accepting that things may not always be what they seem, and it encourages elusiveness and inconclusiveness. In its worst form, irony degenerates into sarcasm and an aloof distancing that kills warmth and intimacy. But irony can also be scintillating and playful and, ironically enough, a sincere means of finding personal meaning in a world of hidden motives and unstable values.

THE MAN WHO FELL TO EARTH

In early summer 1972, David Bowie, a minor pop star who had been trying to make the big time since the mid-'60s, appeared on the BBC music show *Top of the Pops*. Rail-thin with hair dyed carrot red and cut into a modified shag that was neither long nor short and conveyed neither masculinity nor femininity, the pallid musician, starkly contrasted against a pitch-black stage, strummed the opening notes of his new single "Starman" on a blue acoustic guitar.

As the camera pulled back to reveal the singer in a quilted, multicolor spacesuit, Bowie draped a languorous arm around his lead guitarist's shoulder in a louche gesture that decidedly did *not* invoke laddish bonhomie.

This was the TV debut of Bowie's Ziggy Stardust persona — a character he created for what would be his breakthrough release, *The Rise and Fall of Ziggy Stardust and the Spiders from Mars*, a meta-album that tells the story of a fictional band through a pastiche of sounds — heavy metal riffs, hippie acoustic guitar, fractured rock 'n' roll saxophones, doo-wop backing vocals — and lyrics that were light on love and heavy on allusions to fascism, science fiction, death, and the end of the world.

Against the backdrop of British adolescents dancing awkwardly in their '70s earth tones, Bowie/Stardust looked just as he intended: Like some futuristic voyager set down upon a lonely planet, an interstellar rock 'n' roll messiah brought to Earth on a mission to teach the children to boogie.

THE POP-CULTURAL SUPERMARKET

That preceding heroic vignette is offered with tongue somewhat in cheek (but *not* with irony; let's be clear with definitions: facetiousness is not irony, and neither is coincidence — although they are often confused). Nevertheless, sometime near the early '70s, a cultural threshold had undeniably been crossed.

We could just as easily have opened with the premiere of director and screenwriter John Waters' camp masterpiece *Pink Flamingos*, also from

1972. What little plot the movie has revolves around the machinations of two families battling for the title of Filthiest Person Alive. But it's the details that make the movie a classic — motifs lovingly chosen by Waters to cause maximum offense to a typical early 1970s audience: drag, white slavery, drug abuse, bestiality, gore, mental illness, lesbianism, trailer parks, honest-to-God poop eating, and thick, thick Baltimore accents.

At first glance, the self-consciously stylized Bowie-as-Ziggy and the exuberantly profane Waters seem poles apart. However, both were making a sort of cut-and-paste art that jumbled together pop-cultural allusions to make something novel and all but unintelligible to an outsider. *Pink Flamingos* and *Ziggy Stardust* were speaking to a generation of pop-culture connoisseurs, the first to grow up watching TV and listening to teenage Top 40 music, kids who quoted song lyrics and commercial jingles the way people once used to quote Shakespeare and the Bible.

On *Top of the Pops*, David Bowie wasn't David Bowie anymore; he was inhabiting his creation. When John Waters laughed at inner-city schoolkids shooting heroin, he wasn't actually laughing at *them* but at the *idea*, which was largely a fantasy created by the overworked reactionary imagination of frightened suburbanites. He was laughing at "inner-city schoolkids shooting heroin."

The era of irony had begun.

POSTMODERN POP

By 1972, rock music was old enough to have its own history. Glam rock pioneers like David Bowie and (later in the fateful summer of '72) Roxy Music played with that history, tweaking rock conventions to make new music that simultaneously celebrated the music of their youth and lampooned an era that, after the turbulence of the late '60s, seemed quaint and naive. Any social critique, though, was arch, covered in layers of irony. All that heavy-message music of the hippies, after all, was *such* a drag, darling.

As the name implies, glam rockers longed for the Art Deco sophistication of a '30s nightclub, the elegance of Hollywood's golden era, the otherworldly vistas of science fiction, or the unbridled decadence of Berlin on the brink of World War II. In short, anywhere other than the unbearable drabness of the here and now. Where irony goes, nostalgia is often close behind.

This was the moment youth culture became self-aware. Hurried along in their recognition by their music-chart rivals — the singer-songwriters who exuded a painful sincerity — the artier glam acts resoundingly rejected artistic authenticity. Angry Teen Rebel, Poet Truth-Teller, Swaggering Rock 'n' Roll God — all were just personas, useful perspectives from which to make art, but offering no window to the true artist beneath. Art was inherently artifice, and claims of authenticity were nothing more than self-deceiving lies.

This self-reflexive theater of art was the pop manifestation of a philosophical movement that emerged out of the cultural and physical rubble of the Second World War: postmodernism.

INTELLECTUAL IRONY

In light of the murderous nightmare that both communism and fascism had become, of two devastating world wars, of the unparalleled crime of the Holocaust, and of the unending existential threat posed by the Cold War, intellectuals looking toward the closing decades of the twentieth century reasonably enough began to doubt the value of Big Ideas. They adopted a highly critical stance toward systems of all kinds — philosophical, political, scientific — and became particularly fixated on langue, the most pervasive and subtly influential system of them all.

The resulting field of critical theory has been rightly criticized for being intensely self-reflexive, unnecessarily abstruse, and politically disengaged. But to the postmodernists, that was a feature, not a bug: The dangers of acting too quickly had been found to be altogether less salubrious than those of prolonged second-guessing and navel-gazing.

Next to language, postmodernism was most keenly alive to the rise of a consumer culture in which people expressed their identity through purchasing decisions. In a world now connected by the bonds of international capitalism, anything could be acquired from anywhere, and, consequently, nothing seemed authentic any longer. Any word, any image, any object, any sentiment could be prefabricated and potentially concealed as a sales pitch.

For individuals distrustful of institutions, wary of any definitive position, deeply aware of ways discourse and the self are constructed, irony is the natural way of being in the world. And this point of view wasn't limited to philosophers and Marxist intellectuals. In Andy Warhol's iconic silk screens of identical Campbell soup cans and the massively enlarged comic-book images of Roy Lichtenstein's canvases, the pop art of the early '60s simultaneously exposed, ridiculed, and exulted in a culture devoted to mass-producing cheap trash.

CAMPING IT UP

An art school fugitive, Bowie knew his intellectual sources — or at least he could cite them when convenient. John Waters, on the other hand, learned his irony the old-fashioned way: by consuming tremendous amounts of trash culture. Throughout his six decades as a cultural force, Waters has been an unflagging champion of an aesthetic known as *camp*.

This term for a self-conscious yet sincere affection for failed or otherwise bad art was not widely known beyond the gay community before cultural critic Susan Sontag wrote an essay about it in 1964. Rereleased in an anthology in 1966 — the height of the Swinging '60s — "Notes on Camp" made her famous and gave highbrow America a tool for understanding pop-cultural artifacts like *Batman* and *The Wild, Wild West*, TV shows that traded on ridiculously overblown acting and a "so bad it's good" approach to scriptwriting.

The lovable, drunk uncle of postmodernism, camp shares the former's disbelief in authenticity but without any of its academic dourness. Camp is hilarious, dramatic, ridiculous, catty, and — deep down at a place it rarely acknowledges — wounded and humane. While postmodernism observes pop culture in order to critique it, camp luxuriates in it, as if soaking in a champagne-filled bathtub, embellished with gilded angel faces… and little baroque curlicues.

THE '80S: IRONY GOES MAINSTREAM

The camp and irony of the 1970s paraded their own triviality. But that triviality was itself a critique of the failed ambitions of the 1960s. From the bleak perspective of the Nixon era — recession, energy crisis, inflation, Watergate, crime, urban decay — the hippie message of peace and love through drugs and sex seemed painfully naive and shamefully narcissistic.

The fundamental emptiness of David Bowie (or is it "David Bowie"?) was a repudiation of the songwriter-as-activist persona that had been played by musicians like Bob Dylan and John Lennon. And in his cinema tributes to filth, John Waters, far from wanting to change the world, reveled in its brokenness.

There were teeth to that. But by the mid-1980s, irony had been tamed. Television shows like *Saturday Night Live*, Canada's short-lived but influential *SCTV*, and *Late Night with David Letterman* made comedy synonymous with irony. This proliferation reduced irony to a pose, a learned response of cool disaffectedness in the face of anything.

But this didn't just happen on its own. Irony conquered America because it offered a comfort people craved. To the counterculture, it provided a way of mocking a dominant culture that seemed impervious to change. Are you stuck with three networks all making crappy TV? Well, *Dallas* is pretty funny — if you know how to watch it the right way. Is the president illegally funding Central American death squads? Let's go watch those movies he made with that chimpanzee back in the 1950s — that'll be a *total* burn on him.

The most perfect and poignant (and insufferable) ironists, though, were the former hippies themselves, baby boomers who had survived their radical past to become money- and status-driven yuppies. The cognitive dissonance of someone who once clashed with Governor Ronald Reagan over free speech on college campuses and was now — just 12 years later — electing him president must have been staggering. And tax cuts could provide only so much comfort. The living embodiment of this uneasy contradiction — the "social liberal" but "fiscal conservative" — was the ubiquitous BMW-driving lawyer or software engineer who had the daring to wear blue jeans with his blazer and kept his a ponytail as a visual reminder of that ideals of his youth were still alive and well… somewhere.

For this peculiar chimera of the '80s, irony was a second ponytail. It was a sign that he was still hip to it; that no matter what he looked like, in his heart, he was still out there throwing bombs with the people and sticking it to the Man.

This was chemically pure irony: all surface and no substance; saying one thing, but signifying something utterly different indeed. ●

TV CONSOLE GAMES

"I don't want anybody who reads this [proposal] to get turned off.... So the first thing I don't do is call it a toy. But I can call it gaming."

— INVENTOR RALPH BAER, ON HOW
HE DECIDED TO PITCH HIS CONCEPT FOR
THE WORLD'S FIRST TV CONSOLE GAME

TIME OF ORIGIN: *1972*

ORIGIN IN: *Magnavox offices, Fort Wayne, Indiana*

HYPE FACTOR: *4 — The first home video gaming system was actually undermarketed, and it took several years for sales to take off.*

IMPACT FACTOR: *7 — TV now is just another screen, and increasingly it is gaming that people want to see on it.*

When the now-venerable game franchise and perpetual insult to good taste *Grand Theft Auto* was released in its fifth version in the fall of 2013, it grossed a record-smashing $800 million in worldwide sales in a single day — more than any other entertainment product ever. No movie, record, or book (LOL!) had done better.

Just in the year 2013, the global video game industry took in $67 billion; by 2017 that's expected to grow to $82 billion, tantalizingly close to the $94 billion movies earned globally in 2010. Since the Great Recession, the US gaming industry has grown an average of four times faster than the rest of our economy.

Video games are firmly established as a major part of the entertainment industry — economically, at any rate. Culturally, it's a different story. While millions of Americans play *Candy Crush* or solitaire on their smartphones, the popular image of the gamer is still young, male, and distinctly undersocialized.

While this might be an out-of-date stereotype, the Gamergate scandal of 2014 — when a number of female game writers who criticized the homogeneity of video games were threatened in graphically violent and sexualized ways by disgruntled male gamers — is evidence of what might charitably be called growing pains as a niche geek market opens up to become part of mass culture.

The first steps of this process happened more than 40 years ago. Before there were PCs and video arcades, video games entered American life though console boxes plugged into TV sets. This time the revolution was definitely televised.

THE FATHER OF THE VIDEO GAME

Ralph Baer was born in Germany in 1922. In 1938, he and his Jewish family fled to the US just months before the terrors of Kristallnacht. Although his education had been cut short, Baer earned a certification in radio and television repair though a correspondence school. After an interlude in which he was able to give Mr. Hitler a little payback during World War II, Baer went back to school on the G.I. Bill, and in 1949 he became one of the first people in the nation to receive a BS in television engineering.

Baer had gotten in on the television business practically from the ground floor, but already he was looking to the next big thing. In his mind, the obvious next step was to use TV sets interactively instead of just to watch network broadcasts. Tasked with designing a high-end TV in 1955 for the Bronx-based Loral Electronics company, he suggested installing a game system — which of course, didn't exist yet.

"Just build the damn set," his boss told him. "You're behind schedule as it is."

GAMING PREHISTORY

While TV gaming was still more than a decade away in 1955, the earliest computer games to use a graphic display were already being built. But they weren't for play. Computers then were still room-size behemoths with tiny brains and inordinately large price tags. Locked away at research institutions and the largest of companies, they were poorly understood by the public. Demonstrations of games like tic-tac-toe or tennis were good forms of public outreach, and they also were a means of testing the limitation of the machines.

The first foreshadowing of what video games would come, however, was a combat game called *Spacewar!* that originated at MIT in 1962. With an astronomically accurate background and physically correct gravitational modeling, *Spacewar!* had a technical sophistication that wouldn't be matched until the late 1970s. However, since mainframe computers were still rarities, *Spacewar!* was a geeks-only phenomenon confined to the campuses of a handful of research universities.

THE ODYSSEY TO THE ODYSSEY

In 1966, Baer had his self-described eureka moment. While waiting for a colleague at Manhattan's Port Authority Bus Terminal on humid day in late August, Baer, in a flash of inspiration, sketched out his ideas for adapting a television set for game play. Those original notes are gone, but the four pages of notes he drafted at the office the next day on a yellow legal pad are now housed at the Smithsonian Institution — along with the machines that ultimately derived from them.

At first, Baer kept his new project to himself. Running a 500-employee-strong division of a military contractor, Baer was able to quietly divert one or two engineers to work on his pet project. "It was a piece of Jewish chutzpah," he admitted. Once he had made some headway, he went to his superiors. They gave him $2,500 and official permission for his two coworkers to continue helping him — whenever there wasn't more pressing business than developing games.

By 1967, Baer's team had developed TV Game Unit #1 or TVG#1, a box that produced a dot on at TV screen that could be manually controlled by a viewer wielding a joystick. Once they figured out how to put up a second dot, they'd made their first game, the primitive but addictive *Chase*. "It's just two *frigging spots on screen*," Baer later recalled, "and it makes one exciting game."

After a few more years of tinkering and six more prototypes, TVG#1 had developed into a multiplayer, multi-program television game system nicknamed the Brown Box. In 1971, Baer and his employer, Sanders Associates, filed for a patent and then set about trying to market their new device. Setting up meetings with pay television companies and major manufacturers of TV sets, they generated favorable responses but no offers until Magnavox signed a licensing deal.

In 1972, Magnavox released the Odyssey, the first home video game console.

STUMBLING OUT OF THE GATE

Although it is sometimes considered the first home computer, the Odyssey was all hardware. Its 40 transistors and 40 diodes offered a repertoire of a dozen games, including volleyball, handball, soccer, hockey, and Ping-Pong.

The concept was breathtakingly new, but the games themselves were underwhelming, and Magnavox's marketing lacked enthusiasm and vision. Seeing the game system primarily as a gimmick for selling more TV sets, Magnavox strictly controlled distribution and cultivated the misleading impression that the Odyssey worked only on its own brand of sets. It was expensive, too, retailing at $100. In the first year, Magnavox had sold fewer than 130,000 units — hardly a breakthrough success.

THE SECOND TIME'S A CHARM

In the late '60s, while Baer and his team were perfecting their Brown Box in New Hampshire, in the San Francisco Bay Area, 29-year-old computer scientist Nolan Bushnell was trying to market his own version of *Spacewar!* Rather than focus on home TVs, though, Bushnell, a former amusement park employee who was inspired by pinball arcades, was aiming for a coin-operated arcade game. Released several months before the Magnavox Odyssey, Bushnell's *Computer Space* takes the crown as the first commercial video game, but its complex game play attracted few fans.

Nevertheless, Bushnell had tasted enough success to attempt an early Silicon Valley start-up. He wanted to name his company Syzygy, but the arcane astronomical term was already taken, so he settled instead for an arcane term from the Japanese strategy game Go. Atari was started with $500 of Bushnell's money. Early employees included a young Steve Jobs and Steve Wozniak.

FOUNDATIONAL MOMENTS IN GAMING

1952: A.S. Douglas of the University of Cambridge makes the first computer game to use a graphical display. It's a version of tic-tac-toe he programmed on EDSAC, one of the world's earliest computers.

1958: William A. Higinbotham, a physicist who helped develop the first nuclear bomb, uses his brains to make happier history when he becomes the first American to create an interactive computer game, *Tennis for Two*, which he developed to entertain visitors at an open house at Brookhaven National Laboratory in Upton, NY.

1962: Steve Russell and a couple buddies at MIT develop *Spacewar!*, a game that sets the technological benchmark for video games for at least a decade. As two triangular spacecraft engage in a showdown across a central sun, the challenge is to dodge your adversary's weaponry while navigating the sun's gravitational field. Memory limitations of the PDP-1 computer compelled the programmers to exempt the missiles from the effect of the sun's gravitational pull — so they styled them as photon torpedoes, which, as bursts of pure energy, are obviously not affected by gravity — *duh*! *Spacewar* spreads rapidly as open-source software through the underground research-nerd circuit, where it proliferates in countless variants.

1971: Baer files a patent, granted in 1973, that effectively makes any TV-based gaming or training simulation his intellectual property.

1971: Nolan Bushnell creates *Computer Space*, the first commercial video game. In a time before video arcades, the game is set up in bars. Although the game is housed in an ultramodern fiberglass body with a sweet metal-flake finish, its detailed instructions and complex play are well beyond the competence of anybody working on a second piña colada. Accordingly, the game is a failure.

1972: Baer's "Brown Box" console game is released by TV manufacturer Magnavox as the Odyssey gaming system. It features 12 pre-installed games, including Ping-Pong.

1972: Bushnell rebounds from the disaster of *Computer Space*, founds Atari, and releases a much more modest arcade video game: Ping-Pong. *Pong* becomes the first hit video game.

1975: Atari releases *Pong* for TV, is promptly sued by Magnavox for patent infringement, and settles out of court.

1976: *Death Race*, an arcade game whose object is to run down screaming stick figures as they flee for their lives, becomes the first video game to generate moral panic over excessive violence.

1976: Fairchild Video Entertainment System (aka Channel F) becomes the first console game to use a microprocessor rather than dedicated circuits and to have interchangeable game cartridges.

1978: *Space Invaders* causes the biggest sensation since *Pong*; it also represents the first incursion of a Japanese business into video gaming.

1978: In a huge moment for gaming and a major blow to American cuisine, Atari's Nolan Bushnell opens Pizza Time Theatre (now Chuck E. Cheese's) arcade and restaurant.

1980: America is stricken with an epidemic of *Pac-Man* fever. Japanese manufacturer Namco has the distinction of introducing the first video game to have a character with its own name.

1981: Nintendo's *Donkey Kong* introduces beloved character Mario.

1982: Atari's *E.T. The Extra Terrestrial* becomes the first major flop in the TV console industry, a bellwether for disaster to come. Famously, Atari has the unsold games buried in a New Mexico landfill.

1983: Too many competing consoles systems and a glut of crummy games rushed to market lead to a crash, which is exacerbated by the arrival of the PC in the form of the Apple II, Radio Shack's TRS-80, and the Commodore 64.

1984: Magnavox discontinues the Odyssey, and a nearly bankrupt Atari sells off its home electronics division.

1986: Nintendo's NES saves the console game industry and ushers in the modern era of gaming.

At a trade show, Bushnell had discovered the Odyssey. "I thought it was kind of crappy," he was reported as saying. "But I noticed some people were having some fun with it." For Atari's first project, Bushnell directed designer Allan Alcorn to make a Ping-Pong game — without mentioning the source of his inspiration — and adding, quite falsely, that the company had been contracted by General Electric.

Atari's *Pong* was a rip-off, but a much superior rip-off. Play had been improved by tweaking the paddles so that they responded differently according to where they were struck, and the new game also featured a scoreboard and great sound effects.

Atari debuted *Pong* in late 1972 in Sunnyvale, California, at a dive called Andy Capp's Tavern. Within a couple days, the coin box was so full that it jammed. *Pong* was a hit. In several weeks, machine parts were already malfunctioning from overuse. By 1973, Atari was earning $1 million selling *Pong* consoles.

After releasing more successful arcade games, Atari moved into the TV console market with a home version of *Pong*. Magnavox, which had been inactive before, now sued for patent infringement.

A DETENTE, OF SORTS

Atari was making video games that people wanted to play, but Magnavox held the patents. Eventually, the companies struck a compromise out of court: Atari paid $700,000 and in return became a licensee. For the rest of the '70s and into the early '80s, Atari dominated the rapidly growing video game industry, rolling out hit after hit.

Magnavox, for its part, was happy to sue all the newcomers and earn its profits that way. Over the next 20 years, the original TV gaming company would win more than $100 million in court. A vice president of Nintendo and victim of Magnavox's well-exercised legal team was not incorrect when he complained in 1989, "Magnavox isn't in the business of making video games. They're just in the business of suing people."

This wasn't exactly the future that Baer had predicted for his invention. But by 1975 he was out of the video game business anyway. As a private consultant, he developed a number of electronic games, the most successful of which was the memory game *Simon*. Consisting of four glowing wedges that each emitted a unique note, the game plays patterns of ever-increasing complexity that the player must then duplicate. In a delightful twist of fate, Baer had lifted the idea from one of Bushnell's Atari games as brazenly as Bushnell had copied Baer's electronic Ping-Pong. •

METRICATION

"*I look upon our English system as a wickedly brain-destroying piece of bondage under which we suffer. The reason why we continue to use it is the imaginary difficulty of making a change, and nothing else; but I do not think in America that any such difficulty should stand in the way of adopting so splendidly useful a reform.*"

— LORD KELVIN, FROM A LECTURE
DELIVERED IN PHILADELPHIA IN 1884

TIME OF ORIGIN: *1975*

ORIGIN IN: *Washington, D.C.*

HYPE FACTOR: *10 — Advocates created a* Schoolhouse Rock *rip-off! Opponents derided it as a communist plot!*

IMPACT FACTOR: *1 — We are still kilometers and kilometers away from going metric.*

We Americans love to feel exceptional. We take enormous pride in our differences from other nations — from our manifestly remarkable distinctions, such as being the first successful model of a multiethnic liberal democracy, to our less easily understood eccentricities, like our fondness for firearms (and high tolerance for firearms-related deaths).

This unwillingness to adopt the standards of the many also applies to our measurement system: Today, all but three of the world's industrialized nations have adopted the metric system. So it's undeniable that metrication — the process of transitioning to the international decimal system of weights and measures originally devised in revolutionary France — is an example of a phenomenally successful trend. Since, however, the US happens to be one of those lone holdouts, metrication is remembered here as a joke and a failure.

DON'T TREAD ON MY FOOT

In theory, the metric system seems the obvious choice. While the inch and the pound aren't really based on anything, metric units take their standards from nature: Water freezes at zero degrees Celsius and boils at 100; a cubic centimeter of water weighs one gram; and one meter is one ten-millionth the distance from the equator to either pole. Granted, none of that knowledge is particularly helpful when you're trying to measure the house for curtains or bake a cake, but at least it's a rational basis.

The greatest appeal of metric, of course, is that it is a decimal system, so moving between units is a snap — just add or remove some zeros. It's infinitely easier than converting between inches, feet, yards, and miles.

And yet, when theory was put into action, the American public overwhelmingly rejected simplicity and rationality in favor of its unwieldy and arbitrary (but familiar) system of weights and measures.

American exceptionalism triumphed again.

A FOUNDATIONAL MISCALCULATION

In our cultural memory, metrication is inextricably bound to the do-goodery of President Jimmy Carter, a leader whose answer to the skyrocketing fuel prices of the 1977 energy crisis was to appear on national TV wearing a cardigan. But the truth, as it tends always to be, is more complex. Carter may bear the brunt of the shame, but he was simply executing policy that had been proposed under Richard Nixon and signed into law by Gerald Ford.

But if anyone is to blame for America's drawn-out and bungled conversion to the metric system, the facts point squarely in one direction: at the Founding Fathers.

Article 1, section 8 of the Constitution gives Congress the power "To coin Money, regulate the Value thereof, and of foreign Coin, and fix the

Standard of Weights and Measures." The potential for economic chaos of 13 newly minted states each trading in slightly (and sometimes hugely) different measures was alarming enough for George Washington to address it in his first annual message to Congress, in January 1790. Congress responded in classic form: It created a special committee to consider the issue — and then forgot all about it.

Eventually, the secretary of state, a bright young man named Thomas Jefferson, who knew a thing or two about science and math, proposed two alternatives: Continue using traditional British standards, or come up with a new decimal system, such as the one the French were then developing. As it turned out, the Senate was at that moment engaged in delicate negotiations with the British and French precisely over adopting the metric system. Now it was their turn to delay.

One hundred and seventy years later, the US and UK would still be debating metrication.

After three requests, a 44-year wait, and a 33-year repose in the grave, President Washington was finally granted his wish. In 1832, the Treasury Department made an end run around Congress and on its own authority adopted the 36-inch yard, the 7,000-grain pound, the 231-cubic-inch gallon, and the 2,150.42-cubic-inch bushel as the official measures of the land — more or less what we had as subjects to the British Crown.

In other words, our national system of weights and measures represents the triumph of inertia over political paralysis.

"A DECISION WHOSE TIME HAS COME" — NOT!

America had stuck with traditional measures. Meanwhile, the rest of the world was going metric. By the end of the nineteenth century, most of Europe and South America had converted. By the 1950s, much of Asia and Africa had joined them. When the UK finally threw in the towel and went metric in the 1960s, bringing Commonwealth countries Australia and Canada along, it was clear to US lawmakers that history had spoken. In 1968, Congress commissioned a study to test the feasibility of metrication in the United States. The report, which was issued in 1971, was aptly titled *A Metric America: A Decision Whose Time Has Come.*

In 1975, President Ford signed the Metric Conversion Act, establishing the United States Metric Board, the body that would oversee the voluntary transition to the metric system. In retrospect, the terms of the act seem almost designed to fail. There was no timeline, and the USMB had no coercive power. In true let-it-all-hang-out '70s style, each segment and sector of society was left to convert in its own way and at its own pace. The law would just sit back and allow the use of either system — after all, who was it to judge, man? The USMB's only mandate was to plan and coordinate grassroots metrication initiatives.

But there were no grassroots initiatives to coordinate. Metric's only ardent support came from the business and science sectors, which regularly worked across borders and needed the lingua franca of metric. The rest of the nation was split between the apathetic and the apprehensive.

By default, then, the entire national campaign for metrication came down to that most '70s of activities: consciousness-raising. In a vigorous media blitz, the USMB tried to rally enthusiasm for going metric. Television and radio were barraged with pro-metric public service announcements, public school kids were drilled in converting miles into kilometers and kilograms into pounds, and countless column-inches of newsprint were devoted to the feedback loop of asking about and reporting on Americans' feelings about the imminent switch to decimal measures.

In a remarkable, if unintended, rhetorical move, President Ford's signing statement of the Metric Conversion Act heralding the inception of a metric America can equally be read as projecting its demise: "We should learn from this brief history that legislation cannot solve all our problems. Indeed, if the legislation is not founded on public acceptance, it will have less than no effect at all."

THE FIGHT TO SAVE OUR STANDARDS

Metric legislation may have been shown to lack public acceptance, but it certainly did generate an effect: mostly fear and derision. The national information program that was meant to confront and diffuse public unease with metric only increased anxiety. Understanding the metric system was often equated with knowing how to multiply kilometers into miles or divide Fahrenheit to get Celsius. This gave the impression

HOW NOT TO DO PR

Hoping to duplicate the success of the popular *Schoolhouse Rock* cartoons that ran on Saturday mornings, the Metric Board sponsored its own attempt to make education fun: *The Metric Marvels*. These cartoon shorts featured the adventures of Liter Leader, Meter Man, Super Celsius, and Wonder Gram. The fact that you cannot find a single episode of the seven-episode series anywhere online attests to its complete failure to capture the heart and minds of young Generation Xers.

that we'd be forever calculating figures in our head. That when cooking dinner, for instance, we'd need to remember that a cup equals 0.237 liters and a teaspoon 4.93 milliliters — instead of just using tools with both calibrations. Or that we'd have to multiply the kilometers shown on our speedometers by 0.621 to know whether we were breaking the 55-mph speed limit.

Suspicion and misinformation abounded: Would traditional units be outlawed? Could you be fined for ordering a pint of coleslaw? Would Mile High Stadium be forcibly changed to 1.60943-Kilometer Stadium?

These are hardly exaggerations. A frequently repeated accusation during this period of the Cold War was that road signs marked in kilometers would be a threat to national security because they would make it easier for invading Soviet soldiers to find their way around American roadways.

Perhaps the jingoistic note in much anti-metric rhetoric has to do with the historical moment. The height of the metric rollout overlapped with the 1976 observation of the nation's bicentennial. The celebrations lasted for an entire red-white-and-blue year while, in another set of public service announcements, stirring tales from the birth of our nation were distilled into *Bicentennial Minutes* that aired for almost two years.

In this mood of dewy-eyed nostalgia, peculiar bits of Americana were regarded with newfound affection. The irrational inch and unfathomable mile were symbols of our great heritage now under existential threat from a characterless international standard of weights and measures.

At the end of 1977, after a full two years of hype, a Gallup poll reported that 26 percent of the public had still never heard of the metric system.

METRICATION: COMMUNIST PLOT?

At least Dean Krakel, vice president of the National Cowboy Hall of Fame in Oklahoma City and red-blooded American, thought so and put it into writing in a 1976 editorial attempt to rally forces behind his plan to sue the federal government over metrication.

"Metric is definitely Communist.... One monetary system, one language, one weight and measurement system — one world — all Communist! We are playing into Communist hands." He ends with the observation, "I sure don't want to go home to Colorado one of these days and see a sign that says: '90 kilometers to Cripple Creek.'" Yes, Mr. Krakel, the offensive part of that sign would definitely be the "kilometers" part.

Even worse, that minority was two points higher than the 24 percent of Americans who favored its adoption.

It didn't get any easier from there. Metrication was languishing in a slow squeeze, pinned between the fist of hysteria and the palm of indifference. In 1982, Ronald Reagan at last administered the coup de grace, eliminating funding for the USMB. The president cited its lack of authority and his own eagerness to trim the federal budget. •

THE BOOM BOX

"A big part of this hip-hop culture in the beginning was putting things in your face, whether you liked it or not. That was the graffiti, that's like a break-dance battle right at your feet, you know what I'm saying? Or this music blasting loud, whether you like it or not."

— HIP-HOP PIONEER FAB 5 FREDDY

TIME OF ORIGIN: *Late 1970s*

ORIGIN IN: *South Bronx, New York*

HYPE FACTOR: *4 — Whenever you saw a dude with a boom box on TV, you knew something bad was going to go down.*

IMPACT FACTOR: *4 — The boom box is more the symbol of a cultural moment than a seminal piece of technology.*

The boom box was the Humvee of portable music players. It was big and vulgar, built to invade your space and assert the owner as the top dog in any encounter. Maxing out with six speakers, two tape decks, a five-band radio, and elaborate equalizers, all powered by a dozen or more D batteries pumping out 150 decibels of bass-rich sound, the box could sometimes strain the definition of portability too.

Teens everywhere used them as inexpensive car stereos or as a party-in-a-box for beach getaways or visits to the local park. But what cemented the fame of the boom box was its association with hip-hop — a connection vividly asserted in close-up of a JVC RC-M90 that filled the cover of rapper LL Cool J's debut album, 1985's *Radio*. Before rap went mainstream, boom boxes in cities across the nation were the primary means of spreading and even creating the new sound. Everyone might have had one, but the boom box was owned by hip-hop.

BIRTH OF THE BOX

Boom box is not a technical term, so definitions can get blurry. Using generous criteria, though — a handle for portability and a cassette deck that can record directly from the built-in radio — history's first boom box can be identified as the Philips Radio Recorder from 1969. Its single, monaural speaker, however, couldn't deliver much of a sonic blow. It would take the Japanese to put the *boom* in boom box.

Since the mid-'50s, Japan had been competing in the burgeoning portable transistor radio market and had earned a reputation for making products that were smaller and cheaper (in every sense) than the original American versions. But by the '70s, Japanese electronics companies were trying to shed their copycat image and become innovators.

The chief selling points of the transistor radio were novelty and portability — sound quality, not so much. The iconic image of the early '60s teenybopper would not be complete without a hand-size transistor radio, pressed firmly against the ear so that the listener could absorb every feeble nuance of its tinny, low-volume sound. For the Japanese electronics industry, the challenge was to make a portable device with the fidelity of a home stereo system. By the mid-'70s, with the advent of the boom box, they had succeeded.

TAKING IT TO THE STREETS

Although the new portable music device was an international hit, its less respectable nickname *ghetto blaster* is evidence of how closely the boom box became associated with urban black culture. And that perception was not all distortion, since there was no place that took to the boom box more readily and used it to its fullest potential more than the South Bronx in the late '70s and early '80s.

Relatively inexpensive, boom boxes could be acquired more easily than a full stereo. But the appeal went well beyond the low price tag: The portability and ostentatious power of the boom box suited the anarchic, almost apocalyptic mood of the era. A bankrupt New York City was sliding into decay, and none of the five boroughs suffered more than the Bronx, which was plagued by high unemployment and low public services. Slum landlords who couldn't get any paying tenants infamously resorted to burning down their own buildings for the insurance money.

In a place where the police would not respond to robbery calls, noise complaints were laughable. Boom boxes quickly became ubiquitous on the streets, on the subway, in the parks. Owning one conferred status, because it bestowed the power of starting a party at literally any place — even an empty street. More than one boom box enthusiast has described the device as an urban campfire, an improvised place of community and festivity. Also, with literally thousands of models produced in a roughly ten-year period, the boom box became a style accessory. Finding just the right make was a personal statement, just as picking the right style of tennis shoe would be.

But owning a boom box was a responsibility too: Walking the streets blasting your playlist was an assertion of confidence in your musical taste. It was an invitation to critique from fellow cognoscenti and a provocation to those who just didn't get it. Like other displays of bravado, conspicuous boom box play in public was a way of claiming territory.

The implicit aggression of the boom box was not lost on the wider culture. In every TV crime drama and vigilante-praising action film of the era, the boom box became a quintessential feature of the urban troublemaker, along with a denim vest, a switchblade, and a red bandana.

HERALD OF HIP-HOP

The dire circumstances of '70s New York provided the unlikely inspiration for some great art. While mostly white kids in downtown Manhattan were codifying the sonic assault that became punk rock, in the outer boroughs the petty vandalism of graffiti was being honed into an art form, and in the South Bronx a completely new musical genre was starting to emerge.

Party DJs were raiding their parents' soul albums looking for instrumental hooks to sample and turn into break-beat loops that provided a cut-and-paste soundtrack for dancing. Meanwhile, up-and-coming MCs adopted a technique from Jamaican club DJs and started ad-libbing semi-facetious boasts over instrumental mixes. When the DJs and the MCs collided onstage to the delight of the break-dancers (soon to be known commonly as *B-boys* and *B-girls*), hip-hop was born.

While the classic hip-hop kit consists of two turntables, a microphone, and an amp, the boom box was granted an honorary position in the setup. Back when radio wouldn't play hip-hop and performers weren't making records anyway, home tapes, produced and duplicated on boom boxes, were the essential means of disseminating the sounds. Simple editing features on some models also allowed a degree of amateur mixing too. So a dedicated hip-hop fan could record break-beat loops or, through multiple tape-to-tape overdubs, could add layer after layer until his human beat-boxing attained orchestral levels of complexity.

But it was primarily as a tastemaker that the boom box thrived. Each one was its own personalized, mobile pirate radio station. Because most boxes included two tape decks, if you heard something you liked on the street, you could hand over a cassette and get a copy dubbed on the spot. (*Dubbing* is analogue-speak for *ripping*.)

TIME TO FLIP THE TAPE

The boom box became the exciting emblem of the spontaneous eruption of a vibrant street culture — if you were young and musically adventurous. If you were just someone trying to read the paper on the subway ride home after work, it was the symbol of a civic culture gone to hell.

As New York recovered from its '70s slump, the police adopted the so-called broken-windows policy that targeted quality-of-life crimes. Graffiti started disappearing from subways, and noise complaints were acted on. Boom boxes were methodically driven out of the public arena.

The police were aided by changing technology and consumer preference. By the late '80s, CDs were displacing cassette tapes, and the lighter-weight Walkman was now the musical fetish object. The sonic campfire of the boom box was replaced by the private soundtrack of the personal music player. •

THE WALKMAN

"Walkin' about with a head full of music,
Cassette in my pocket and I'm gonna use it:
Stereo out on the street you know,
oh-oh oh-oh-oh whoa whoa whoa. *"*

— CLIFF RICHARD, FROM THE 1981
UK TOP 10 HIT "WIRED FOR SOUND"

TIME OF ORIGIN: *June 1979*

ORIGIN IN: *Tokyo*

HYPE FACTOR: *8 — Spontaneously, the entire world decided that it wanted a Walkman.*

IMPACT FACTOR: *8 — The Walkman made it okay to wear headphones in public. Honestly, only real weirdos used to do that.*

It was a revolution in portable sound technology that spooked the music industry. Its streamlined styling and intuitive operation taught the world to appreciate sophisticated design. It was wearable technology that became a fashion statement. It was a technological must-have whose speed of adoption was rivaled only by the television and the radio.

Apple's iPod may have transformed headphone culture, but it was the Sony Walkman that invented it.

Measuring 5.5 inches long by 3.5 inches wide and an inch thick, the 14-ounce device was not exactly palm size, but this headphones-only personal music system was a world away from the very obtrusive boom boxes that dominated the portable market in the late 1970s. Music now moved inward, from a collective experience to an individual one, as people started tuning out from one another in public to lose themselves in their individual soundtracks.

From roller-discoing along Venice Beach to jogging in Central Park to aerobicizing at the local Y, the Walkman set the tempo for a nation on the move, and it became *the* iconic device of the 1980s.

A TAPE RECORDER THAT DOESN'T RECORD

The Walkman was a brilliant consumer product. Once you owned one, it seemed so obvious, so inevitable, that you wondered why no one had invented it sooner. And they easily could have. By the late 1970s, a compact portable cassette-tape player was hardly a technological challenge; the components had been around for nearly two decades. In fact, Sony executive deputy president Norio Ohga dismissed the Walkman idea as "boring technologically"; he preferred the sexier challenge of perfecting the compact disc.

In the long run, Ohga was right about digital music. But he and countless other electronics executives around the world had overlooked what existing technology was failing to deliver in the here and now: portability and choice. From the start, the chief obstacle to the Walkman was conceptual: It required letting go of entrenched notions of what cassette tape technology was all about.

Back in the '70s, tape players were universally known as "tape *recorders.*" That's how essential their recording feature was considered. Aside from bulky and difficult-to-operate reel-to-reel tapes, cassettes were the only means of capturing sound at home. Beyond this great virtue, however, cassette tapes kind of sucked. They had a hissy background and narrow dynamic range. With every play, the metal coating that magnetically encodes the sound was abraded as the tape passed over the tape head, so heavy listening would eventually wear out your favorite song. Chances were, however, that a cassette tape would get eaten by the player — snarled in the inner workings of capstans, levers, and springs — twisted and creased through casual mishandling, or demagnetized by being left on top of a speaker well before it had the chance to wear out.

When they entered the market in the early '60s, cassettes were considered a convenient, disposable, lo-fi sound technology that was immensely useful for secretaries and journalists but entirely unsuitable for music. In practice, however, portability proved irresistibly seductive. Since the cassette could go where vinyl couldn't, people on the go started listening to music on tape, and they were amply willing to sacrifice quality for convenience. By the '70s, tape decks were a common sight in car dashboards and provided an essential element in the trendy portable radio-cassette player. [See **The Boom Box**]

IT WAS ALMOST THE *WALKY*

Success, as the cliché goes, has many fathers, and the Walkman is no exception. According to the Sony website, the impetus came from honorary chairman Masaru Ibuka, who wanted to listen to classical music during his frequent international business flights; however, *Time* magazine claims that Ibuka himself credited CEO Akio Morita, who wanted to listen to music on the tennis court. (The *New Yorker*'s source at Sony makes the more plausible case that Morita ordered the headphones-only device so he wouldn't have to overhear his teenage kids' music.) Yet another version is that engineers from Sony's tape division came up with the prototype when they were messing around with a previously existing transcription recorder, because that's the sort of thing engineers do for fun.

Whoever conceived of the Walkman, it was Morita who recognized the potential market for a personal stereo and made the new product a global phenomenon. In February 1979, Morita ordered his tape recorder division to develop a high-fidelity, playback-only, headphone stereo. The target would be students, so the price had to be under ¥40,000 (about $200) and it had to be ready to go by the start of summer vacation, now four months away. The division delivered on everything, just ten days behind schedule.

One of the team's most insoluble problems was what to name the product they had been developing as model number TPS-L2. Since it was based on the design of an earlier device marketed as the Pressman, the engineers started calling the cassette player the *Walkman*. But Morita rejected the name. He thought it sounded like a ham-fisted Japanese attempt to use English — which it was. But no one could come up with anything better, so *Walkman* it was. At least for the domestic market. The TPS-L2 would be sold as the Soundabout in the US, the Stowaway in the UK, and as the Freestyle in Sweden.

Once the Walkman caught on in Japan, however, its fame spread so quickly that international consumers knew the name before they could even buy the product. *Walkman* stuck. And Morita was stuck with a name he hated.

COOL HUNTING

Sony was attempting to create a "headphone culture" almost from scratch, so it released the Walkman amid an advertising blitz designed to portray the Walkman as youthful, cool, and a radical break from the past. One early ad shows a Buddhist monk with clumsy, old-school headphones frowningly regarding the leggy embodiment of early '80s femininity — leg warmers, high heels, strapless leotard, sweater sportily knotted around the waist — uninhibitedly boogieing to the sounds of her prominently displayed Walkman.

The product preview for the press emphasized portability and speed, and included exhibitions of roller skaters, skateboarders, and even a man and woman riding a tandem bicycle — each tuned in to his or her own funky soundtrack, thanks to Sony's revolutionary new player.

Despite the hoopla, the press was unimpressed, and the first month's sales were a sluggish 3,000 units. But consumers quickly perceived the Walkman's appeal. By the end of the summer, the entire initial run of 30,000 had sold out. By the end of 1980 — several months after the Walkman's global release — sales hit two million.

A MUSIC-CULTURE CLASH

When the Walkman hit the US in June 1980, it was instantly a hit — and was immediately deployed in our long-running culture wars.

The Wall Street Journal fired one of the first shots, in a June 23 article that ran under the headline "New Cassette Player Outclasses Street People's 'Box.'" *Outclasses*, here, was offered as both a technical and a social judgment. While avoiding the terms *hip-hop* and *punk*, the piece sneeringly portrays the typical boom box aficionado as the sort of person who carries "a knife in one pocket and a zip gun in the other." The Walkman, on the contrary, is the "middle- and upper-class answer to the box" and "one of the hottest new status symbols" for "the smart set." Pop artist and arbiter of hip Andy Warhol was an early adopter, as were sex kittens Britt Ekland and Suzanne Somers, tennis legend Björn Borg, and musicians such as Paul Simon and Todd Rundgren.

A representative of Bloomingdale's, *the* place where Manhattan's glitterati went to acquire the new fetish object, is quoted as saying that owning a

Walkman was "like belonging to the club of Mercedes Benz owners.... When you see each other, you nod." A *New York Times* article from July presents a similar quotation, this time attributed to a Central Park stroller who sports his Walkman from a Gucci belt.

The '80s... *ugh!*

But the Walkman wasn't just for celebrities and insufferable yuppies. If it had been divisive at first, headphone culture soon cut across every subset of American life, from commuters relaxing to Barry Manilow to their teenage kids getting off the wall with Michael Jackson, from junkies on the subway to frightened tourists. The flood hit so quickly and thoroughly that in late 1981 the *New Yorker* devoted more than two columns simply to documenting the diversity of Walkman users spotted across the breadth and length of the nation. Even the boom box demographic was eventually won over to the lighter and more mobile newcomer.

The numbers bear out the Walkman's sweeping effect: In 1981, vinyl albums outsold cassettes five to three; in 1982, the numbers were even. For the rest of the decade, cassettes would outsell albums, until they too were surpassed by CDs, in the early '90s. Sales of blank cassettes also soared, from 180 million in 1982 to 250 million in 1986 as portable cassette wearers perfected the art of the mixtape. The Walkman is even credited with spurring the fitness trend by luring people onto their feet: Between 1987 and 1997, the number of Americans who walked for exercise jumped by 30 percent.

Then came the ultimate sign of cultural arrival: In 1986, the word *Walkman* was added to the *Oxford English Dictionary*.

A CLASSIC RETIRES

Although the Walkman is barely a shadow of the behemoth it once was, it still endures, and it has changed with the times. In all, Sony has rolled out more than 300 models — some included radios, others boasted "bass boost" and auto-reverse features, others still were waterproof or solar powered. Later models played CDs, minidiscs, or even DVDs. Indeed in 2014, Sony courted audiophiles with the Walkman NW-ZX2, a hi-def audio digital player with a touchscreen, wi-fi, and 128 gigabytes of storage. One can be yours for a mere $1,200. Initially however, Sony was slow to adopt the MP3 format, and that misstep allowed Apple's audio player to usurp the portable music market away from the company that created it.

In late 2010, Sony discontinued the cassette Walkman in Japan. That was the same year that the *Oxford English Dictionary* added another word from sound technology: *iPod.* ●

PROZAC

"Prozac has attained the familiarity of Kleenex and the social status of spring water."

— NEWSWEEK, FEBRUARY 6, 1994

TIME OF ORIGIN: *1988*

ORIGIN IN: *Eli Lilly and Company, Indianapolis*

HYPE FACTOR: *9 — The only thing Americans like more than indulging in self-help hype is judging others for indulging in self-help hype.*

IMPACT FACTOR: *8 — On the plus side, we now perceive depression and other mental illnesses as simply that — mental illnesses, which can be treated with a pill. But, on the downside, we now believe that mental illnesses can be treated with just a pill.*

Before Prozac hit the pharmacies, many Americans regarded depression as something frightening and shameful. And their opinion of psychoactive medication — shaped by images of the tic-wracked, zombified asylum inmates of 1975's Best Picture–winning *One Flew over the Cuckoo's Nest* — was even worse.

But a little green and white pill shattered those perceptions. By 1994, the year of peak Prozac, millions of depressed Americans had outed themselves and were proudly riding the medication wave. And millions more on the sidelines regarded them, for the first time, with something approaching envy. *Where's* my *personality pill?*

But they weren't ignored for long. Prozac — along with the flood of personality-enhancing drugs to follow and the endless stream of books and TV commentary — promulgated the idea that we are merely walking chemical reactions in a suit of skin. A tweak here, a boost there, and one day we might have the personality we always knew we deserved. "Cosmetic psychopharmacology" would fulfill in a quite literal way the promise of better living through chemistry.

Today, as many as one in five Americans regularly take psychiatric medication to treat a roster of compulsions and bothersome emotions that includes — but is by no means limited to — depression, anxiety, shyness, panic attacks, eating disorders, smoking, drinking, and grief.

While it might be legitimate to question whether we are overmedicating ourselves, one area where Prozac deserves unqualified praise is how it's managed to change cultural attitudes so quickly and so thoroughly. Depression and anxiety are no more stigmatized now than are heart disease and asthma.

INTO THE GAP

To understand how Prozac came to be, let's start by revisiting the 1936 Nobel Prize for Physiology or Medicine. That year the honor was shared by two scientists, Sir Henry Dale of England and the Austrian Otto Loewi, who had been independently studying how neural impulses are transported across synapses, the gap between nerve cells. Scientists had assumed that electricity did the job, but the pair demonstrated that it was actually chemicals that ferried the information. The first so-called neurotransmitter to be discovered was acetylcholine, which tells a muscle that the brain wants it to contract. Many others were to follow.

Throughout the 1950s, experiments in Europe and the US with drugs that affected neurotransmitters in humans showed an often unlooked-for effect on mood. One trial in Switzerland's evocatively named Münsterlingen asylum demonstrated that the drug imipramine had a stimulating effect on schizophrenics. That was certainly *not* what the clinicians were looking for in this case; however, they reasoned, the imipramine lift might be just the thing for depressives.

Under the brand name Tofranil, imipramine entered the marketplace in 1958. It was the first antidepressant and the first of what would soon be a growing class of drugs called *tricyclics*.

WORSE THAN THE DISEASE?

Tofranil was effective — mitigating symptoms in 60 to 80 percent of patients. But Tofranil, and the other tricyclics that followed it, had serious side effects. Patients commonly felt sluggish and cloudy headed. Weight gain was common, as were constipation and other irritations such as dry mouth, sexual dysfunction, and increased sweating. Worst of all, tricyclics are difficult to dose correctly: too little, and they won't work; too much, and a patient can die. Close monitoring by a doctor was imperative, so these antidepressants worked best with hospitalized patients.

A genuine breakthrough in psychotherapy, the tricyclics were hailed as miracle drugs. But the side effects were so severe that medication was warranted in only the worst cases. For the millions who suffered from major or long-term depression but were high-functioning enough to hold their lives together, there was no relief.

THE SECOND COMING

Tricyclics work by increasing the presence of neurotransmitters. They don't actually produce the chemicals; what they do instead is inhibit the neurons' ability to absorb and neutralize — to "reuptake" — what the body mistakenly considers an excess. Tricyclics inhibit the reuptake of a number of neurotransmitters, chief among them serotonin and norepinephrine. While it was clear that this was the secret to their success, it was equally apparent that indiscriminate neurochemical manipulation was also responsible for the side effects. Too little was known of neurotransmitters, though, for scientists to tell which to target and which to leave alone.

That is until researchers at pharmaceutical firm Eli Lilly began to see a correlation between low levels of serotonin and high rates of depression. Even better for them, they had a drug, fluoxetine, that specifically targeted serotonin. The result was the first selective serotonin reuptake inhibitor, or SSRI, an antidepressant that was as effective as the tricyclics but with many fewer side effects.

Eli Lilly knew they were on to something really big. Public opinion on psychotherapeutic medication was changing. Three decades of tricyclics had acclimated patients to the idea that personality problems like depression and anxiety could be chemically treated. And long-term trends in psychology had been pushing toward a more medicalized view of mental illness. There was every reason to expect not only that the currently medicated would the switch to Prozac but that there was also a whole new market waiting to be tapped.

The 1988 launch of Prozac was preceded by a massive advertising blitz that barraged doctors with Prozac pens, posters, and pamphlets. An analysis predicted that Eli Lilly might earn up to $175 million by 1990. The projection fell far short: By 1989, Prozac had earned $350 million — more than the *entire* antidepressant market just two years earlier. More than half a million prescriptions were being written every month. By the early '90s, Prozac was earning more than $1 billion every year.

"BETTER THAN WELL"?

Now, all that came *before* the Prozac hype really hit.

In 1993, psychiatrist Peter Kramer published his account of the remarkable transformations Prozac had worked on a "substantial minority" of people he had treated. These were patients who, in the words of Dr. Kramer, "became 'better than well,' patients who acquired extra energy and became socially attractive." *Listening to Prozac* spent four months on the *New York Times* best-seller list and became one of the year's most talked-about and controversial books.

Kramer made Prozac a household name and, as at least one critic put it, he was its messiah. It was a characterization that Kramer resented. And, to his credit, Kramer did not ignore Prozac's many, sometimes quite serious, side effects. His book stresses the limited number of his Prozac achievers, and frequently questions the advisability of permanent medication as well as the morality of redefining normal emotional conditions as problems to be eradicated. Nevertheless, it is also fair to say that Dr. Kramer didn't exactly grapple with these problems extensively — so it's understandable that, for the tens of thousands who read his book or heard any of his innumerable morning talk show appearances, the message was: *Sure, I might feel a little jittery, but I could FEEL BETTER THAN I EVER HAVE BEFORE.*

That Kramer was also responsible for coining the term *cosmetic psychopharmacology* didn't help endear him to the more cautious and sober members of the medical profession. A highly critical *L.A. Times* op-ed attacked the term as a "glib and inaccurate catchword."

Listening to Prozac had a tremendously galvanizing — and polarizing — effect on the public. Would-be earlier adopters, looking for an edge in business or bump in the social scene, sought out amenable physicians with loose prescription pads; while on the other hand, moral scolds fulminated about our culture of convenience, and worrywarts speculated that we were medicalizing away our humanity, pathologizing profound aspects of being. *What*, they fretted, *would have happened to Van Gogh on Prozac?*

In 1994, the book-length retort to the antidepressant hype, *Talking Back to Prozac*, hit the bookstores, and so did the confessional memoir *Prozac Nation*. On *Oprah*, the *Today* show, *Good Morning America*, *Charlie Rose*, and in all the major magazines and newspapers, Prozac and the medicating of America were debated. For every medical miracle, there was a counterexample of a formerly peaceable soul turned violent or suicidal on Prozac, of side effects far worse than advertised, or of philosophical Prozac refuseniks who had quit the drug, preferring to battle their demons rather than medicate them away.

AFTER THE STORM

A quarter century later, the SSRI debate has not changed much, but it has grown much quieter. Although there is anecdotal evidence that Prozac can make patients violent or suicidal, there is no medical consensus; and while there are indisputably people for whom SSRIs have indeed been miraculous, there are also studies that suggest antidepressants are no more effective than placebos. There is even significant evidence that suggests depression is not actually caused by low serotonin levels.

At this point, though, SSRIs have assumed an inevitability, like automobiles or cocktails — we know they have their downsides, but we willingly use them because the benefits are just too damned seductive. ●

THE END
OF HISTORY?

"What we may be witnessing is not just the end of the Cold War… but the end of history as such: that is, the end point of mankind's ideological evolution and the universalization of Western liberal democracy as the final form of human government."

— POLITICAL SCIENTIST FRANCIS FUKUYAMA,
"THE END OF HISTORY?" 1989

TIME OF ORIGIN: *Summer 1989*

ORIGIN IN: The National Interest *magazine*

HYPE FACTOR: *7 — C'mon, the end of history, you're curious, right?*

IMPACT FACTOR: *3 — History really hadn't ended.*

As the imminent collapse of the Soviet Union became more and more assured during the late 1980s, a barrage of self-congratulating analysis started appearing in media outlets throughout the triumphant West: Just who had struck the lethalest blow and been the most awesomest champion for democracy — cowboy/grandpa Ronald Reagan, steel-spined UK prime minister Margaret Thatcher, or huggable rock star Pope John Paul II? Mr. Reagan, *duh*! But the others had been *totally* rad, too! That's more or less a direct quote from the *Wall Street Journal*.

But there was one piece of commentary that towered above the rest — just as Uncle Sam had loomed over the Berlin Wall and reduced it to rubble with the twitch of a forefinger — an article that epitomized the spirit of the moment and whose title became a rhetorical spiking of the football: "The End of History?"

THE DAY HISTORY DIED

The most important article of 1989 was penned by an obscure political scientist and State Department employee, Francis Fukuyama, and appeared in the summer issue of a neoconservative Washington policy journal called *The National Interest.*

Within weeks the think piece had become the buzz among D.C. opinion makers, and soon after, Fukuyama fever swept the media: first *Newsweek,* then *Time*, the BBC, and all the major newspapers. Fukuyama was interviewed on national TV and profiled in the *New York Times Magazine*, his article translated into Japanese, Italian, Dutch, Icelandic…

Riding the hype, the 36-year-old bookish policy wonk signed a deal to expand his 16-page article into a 464-page book — and drop the question mark from the end of the title.

The provocative — even absurd — claim of Fukuyama's article generated plenty of derision. *Time* called "The End of History?" "the Beginning of Nonsense." Even many old-style conservatives were unimpressed by Fukuyama's argument and methodology. But they did enjoy his publicity. And in the opinion wars, annoying your enemy can be as valuable as out-arguing them.

MR. HEGEL GOES TO WASHINGTON

In all the hype, of course, few who held an opinion of Fukuyama's article had actually read it. The foreign-policy junkies who went beyond the title were almost universally surprised to find that the thesis was directed at a relatively minor dispute in nineteenth-century German philosophy.

In brief, Fukuyama's contention was this: Karl Marx, author of *The Communist Manifesto* (1848) and the intellectual father of the Soviet Union, had derived his view of history from the work of the earlier philosopher G. W. F. Hegel. According to Hegel (according to Fukuyama), our latent intellectual framework — our ideology — shapes the way we see reality so profoundly that it's fair to say that ideology *constitutes* our reality. History, therefore, at its most fundamental level, is the dialectical pendulum swing of ideologies reacting to, supplanting, and, eventually, falling to other ideologies, until just one is left standing.

Once you've found that soundest of ideologies, *then* you can get around to the details of actually dealing with reality and fixing problems like poverty, hatred, and injustice. But that stuff isn't history; it's just housekeeping.

Marx predicted that history would end in the workers' revolution and the realization of the communist ideal of voluntary collaboration and collective property. For defenders of liberal democracy, however, the end point was… well, liberal democracy. And since the Soviet Union had failed, that meant democracy wins! History is *over*, people! QED.

LIFE AFTER HISTORY

For those of us whose concept of history exceeds Hegel's narrowly technical limits, Fukuyama's argument was a meager bone to gnaw on. Sure, communism was dead and buried, but could the present blend of capitalism and democracy really be *it*, the indisputable pinnacle of political possibility? And what about the manifest injustices within democratic nations? Were these fights to end poverty and discrimination not worthy of the term *history*?

Yes and *yes*, according to Fukuyama.

But he did hasten to acknowledge the concerns of his opponents and confess that, to a degree, he shared them. Fukuyama forecasted that religious sectarianism, ethnic prejudice, and even toxic nationalism might perturb the planet — might take decades or even centuries to quell. History wasn't over *everywhere*, after all, just in the West. The rest of the world might take some time to catch up.

Looking closer to home, Fukuyama argued that economic inequality could lead to unrest. So could prejudice and political corruption, at least theoretically. Fukuyama himself denied that either was a significant factor in the US.

In the long arc of what used to be called history, therefore, the game was as good as won. *No need to worry; it'll all turn out fine in the end.* Of course, in the end, all of today's unemployed, all the sick and uninsured, everyone denied the right to marry or to vote will also be dead. But they should rest easy in the knowledge that, at some point in the future, fewer people will have to suffer as they have had to. Besides, just imagine how bad they *would* have had it if they hadn't been living in a market-friendly, right-of-center democracy. Look at what happened to the Soviet Union, after all.

HISTORY NOSTALGIA

Fukuyama may have been the first cock to crow at the faint dawning of the first, strange new day after history stopped, but he wasn't a happy prophet. "The end of history will be a very sad time," he concludes. "The struggle for recognition, the willingness to risk one's life for a purely abstract goal, the worldwide ideological struggle that called forth daring, courage, imagination and idealism, will be replaced by economic calculation, the endless solving of technical problems, environmental concerns and the satisfaction of sophisticated consumer demands."

Imagine a world where no one even bothers to kill or die for an idea; where there's nothing to test our ingenuity except possibly existential (but sadly not ideological) threats like global warming and super-bacteria; no challenge of our moral fiber beyond caring for our families and ensuring that all other families are similarly provided for.

What a waste. What a sad, sad waste that would be. •

NC-17

"I can't see where anything in our film is more destructive to the human spirit than the sort of mindless violence [the Motion Picture Association of America] do approve for children."

— ACTRESS HELEN MIRREN, DEFENDING
THE COOK, THE THIEF, HIS WIFE, AND
HER LOVER AGAINST ITS X RATING

TIME OF ORIGIN: *1990*

ORIGIN IN: *MPAA headquarters, Washington, D.C.*

HYPE FACTOR: *4 — Anything that makes it easier to see boobs will get lots of press coverage.*

IMPACT FACTOR: *2 — Adults-only ratings won't work because grown-ups don't go to the movies anymore.*

It seems like such a no-brainer: a movie rating for adult content. That way, artsy-fartsy filmmakers won't have to dumb down their content, and action-superhero-combat-explosion-seeking teens will instantly know which sleep-inducing talkfests to avoid. Win-win! After all, adults deserve quality entertainment too, right?

Wrong.

First, adults don't go to the movies. At least not in numbers that justify their having a whole rating all to themselves.

Second, it's a well-known fact that "adult content" means just one thing: porn.

THE FLEETING IDEALISM OF THE X RATING

In the late 1960s, the Motion Picture Association of America devised a rating system that could expand content by allowing films to target specific audiences. After a few tweaks, the MPAA settled on the now familiar G, PG, and R ratings, as well X, which indicated content unsuitable for children. Until that point, movies had been subject to the so-called Hays Code, a restrictive set of guidelines originally formulated in the 1930s, banning, among other things, open-mouthed kissing, profanity, and graphic violence. In the wake of the turbulent '60s, that all seemed timid and old-fashioned. The new rating system was touted as a means of allowing filmmakers greater freedom of artistic expression.

In truth, though, the MPAA wanted as little connection as possible with adult-only entertainment. The only rating the association did not bother to copyright was X. So while a G, PG, or R rating could only be awarded by the MPAA, anyone could use X. And that's exactly what the burgeoning porn industry did, proudly flaunting the X and hyperbolic XXX ratings to advertise its particular strain of adult content, which was noticeably light on existential themes and social critique but big on the idea of free love.

Almost immediately the X rating became hopelessly tainted. To date, one of the first X-rated movies, 1969's *Midnight Cowboy*, remains the only member of its class to have won an Academy Award.

So much for risk-taking adult fare.

NC-17: COULD VIOLENCE AND NUDITY BY ANY OTHER NAME BE SO ARTY?

Although there would be a handful of high-profile X-rated films, for the most part directors remained within the limits of an R — or they faced the difficult choice of releasing their films without a rating. Foregoing an MPAA rating was a risky move. Newspapers and TV stations would not advertise unrated and X-rated movies, and many theaters refused to show them.

But in the '80s, a spate of provocative films pushed the edges so hard that the rating system finally broke.

The controversy surrounding the 1986 release of *Blue Velvet* signaled the coming clash. Director David Lynch's masterpiece of creepy-comical surreality received an R rating, which many felt was too light for its disturbing content, which included drug abuse, domestic abuse, voyeurism, a gruesome head wound, and an ant-infested severed ear.

But the dam broke in 1989, when three high-profile films chose no rating over the MPAA's proposed X: the earnest and surprisingly dull *Henry: Portrait of a Serial Killer*, the dark romantic comedy *Tie Me Up! Tie Me Down!* by critically acclaimed Spanish director Pedro Almodóvar, and the intensely arty and just plain intense *The Cook, the Thief, His Wife, and Her Lover*.

In the resulting media storm, the MPAA was lambasted for hypocrisy (it was fine with violence and nudity in a blockbuster like *Conan the Barbarian* but not in a boutique art film) and its questionable standards for questionable content (the MPAA objected to the sexual content of *Tie Me Up! Tie Me Down* but not to its pervasive misogyny).

All three films lost their appeals, but they made their point. In 1990, the MPAA replaced the X rating with NC-17: *Not suitable for children, no one under 17 admitted.* In the fall of that year, the romantic drama *Henry and June* became the first NC-17 movie.

But the "adult content" rating, rebranded and under MPAA control, did little to please anyone. To concerned citizens, smut was smut, no matter how you labeled it. While television and some newspapers were more open to the new rating, many publications would still not advertise NC-17 movies, and many theaters would not show them. Blockbuster, Kmart, and Walmart, which accounted for half of all video sales, refused to stock these titles.

Even backed by a major studio, an NC-17 film could expect to open at fewer than half the number of theaters as a major release. Conventional wisdom held that the typical NC-17 film would play at about 300 theaters and turn a profit of $3 million — chump change by Hollywood standards.

By the mid-'90s, the NC-17 furor had died down, partially because audiences had come to accept it, but mostly because Hollywood became less interested in attracting the NC-17 crowd. As foreign box office started to count more than domestic earnings, economics pushed for plot-light, action-heavy films that would translate easily. Adults seeking challenging content had to look elsewhere.

MORE THAN JUST NAKED PEOPLE

Unrated, X-Rated, and NC-17 films actually worth watching:

Midnight Cowboy (1969): A gritty, funny, and unbearably sad portrait of a pair of street hustlers trying to make their way in a New York City that's starting to seriously feel the hangover from the Swinging '60s.

A Clockwork Orange (1971): Set in a dystopian future, where street-wandering bands of "droogs" practice acts of "ultraviolence" while listening to classical music, the film is often criticized for glorifying the violence it purports to condemn. Wherever you come down on them, however, the questions it raises are serious, and it is a beautifully made film.

The Cook, the Thief, His Wife, and Her Lover (1989): Some 25 years after its release — unrated in theaters and as the first NC-17 video — this film has not lost its power to shock. Stylish, stylized, and staged like a baroque painting, it achieves the feeling of a seventeenth-century revenge play transported to some London-like city in a possible near future. The film drives home its critique of the values fostered by a society of unbound consumerism in a decidedly *un*metaphorical and brutal way, but remains exquisite throughout.

Henry and June (1990): The first NC-17 movie in theaters, it deserves its place in history — although it's the fluffiest film on this list. This enjoyable costume drama portrays the relationship, both artistic and romantic, between authors Anaïs Nin and Henry Miller in 1930s Paris. A controversial-for-the-era lesbian theme is probably what prompted the MPAA to consider this "adult" material.

WHENCE NC-17?

In 2010, NC-17 briefly flared up in public consciousness once more when *Blue Valentine*, starring Ryan Gosling and Michelle Williams, had to fight for an R rating. The media coverage was like a '90s flashback. There was the same outrage at the MPAA's hypocrisy and baffling standards. Gosling accused the organization of being prudish about female sexuality.

But this time around, the controversy glowed with the feeble intensity of a single glow stick at a midnight rave. Twenty years after the introduction of NC-17, the whole MPAA rating system seemed as quaint as the Hays Code had in the late '60s. The change was cable television. Sometimes graphic but always smart and challenging, series like *The Sopranos*, *Deadwood*, and *Breaking Bad* were catering to the adult audience the movies had given up on.

Today, with just a few years' more perspective, NC-17 films can look downright tame: Any given episode of *Game of Thrones* can rival even the brutal decadence of *The Cook, the Thief, His Wife, and Her Lover.* ●

SMART DRINKS

"It's like Cheerios with a chemical-pill aftertaste."

— RAVE-GOER AND SMART-DRINK TASTER
SPEAKING TO THE *L.A. TIMES* IN 1992

TIME OF ORIGIN: *Early 1990s*

ORIGIN IN: *The West Coast rave scene*

HYPE FACTOR: *2 — This was big news if you were a club-goer in the 1990s; otherwise, not so much.*

IMPACT FACTOR: *1 — It created a whole new class of specialty beverage, which is big news if you're in the food industry; otherwise, not so much.*

The rave scene of the 1990s was generous in its supply of mockable trends — many of which are now long forgotten, like those awful baggy, baggy pants, or like putting smiley faces on everything, or wearing surgical masks smeared with Vicks VapoRub on the inside. (Don't even ask....) One folly, however, that has managed to outlive raves — but not its own power to induce eye rolls — is a class of heavily sweetened, amino-acid- and vitamin-enhanced concoctions known today in the food industry as "functional beverages," but referred to back in the day as "smart drinks."

DESIGNER CHEMICALS FOR A DESIGNER BRAIN

Although it was pioneered on the beaches of Ibiza and in a handful of clubs and abandoned warehouses in London and Manchester in the 1980s, rave found its spiritual home a few years later in coastal California. With the goal of producing an ecstatic experience through dancing to electronically produced percussive rhythms (and by ingesting copious quantities of the drug MDMA), the techno-tribal aspect of the rave scene found an especially sympathetic audience in the San Francisco Bay Area during the early days of the first tech boom.

In the clubs that dotted San Francisco's then decidedly un-gentrified SoMa district, drug-consciousness rhetoric of the '60s merged with cyberculture utopianism. Even as processor speeds were doubling and doubling again, acid and ecstasy gurus were predicting a parallel breakthrough in human consciousness — facilitated by the right mix of psychopharmacological additives. From there sprang a minor trend for mixing dietary supplements into sickeningly sweet, Day-Glo-colored, nonalcoholic drinks that were sold at raves with vague promises of sharpening your focus, speeding your thoughts, or energizing your dance moves.

These "smart cocktails" quickly edged out real cocktails, for, according to the neo-hippie peace-and-love ethos of the rave, alcohol was aggro and uncool. It was poison that killed your brain and liver. Cynics, however, suspected that, for all the hype, smart drinks were nothing more than a strategy for selling shots of water for four bucks to dancers tripping too hard on ecstasy to care about an alcohol buzz.

The cynics were right. The November 1992 issue of *Discover* magazine offered an amusing takedown of the smart-drink hype. Their conclusion: You'd get as much energy from drinking coffee and better nutrition simply by eating well. As for the taurine, choline, and other exotic amino acids: "It's an expensive contribution to your bowel movement."

BREAKING NEWS: SMART DRINKS STILL UNDEAD

Lest you suspect the *Discover* article was the ill-informed opinion of some hater who didn't "get" the cognitive revolution, *Wired* magazine, the arbiter of computer culture before it learned to cut the cord, flat-out dismissed smart drinks, listing the craze as number four on its 1993 debut hype list. *Wired* re-proclaimed the death of the fad in 1995… and again in 1997.

Rave culture didn't make it much past Y2K (that's the year 2000, for you analogue dinosaurs) and the nightclub smart-drink bar died with it.

But the raver's drink of choice has continued to live from beyond the grave. In fact, it's thrived.

In the form of enhanced waters and energy drinks, the spawn of the smart drink comprise a significant slice of the functional-beverage market, a $26 billion industry that also includes your yogurt drinks, coconut waters, pre-brewed white teas, and kombuchas.

True to form, the new breed of enhanced waters is also mostly hype. Feeling the pressure of a lawsuit, Pepsi admitted in 2013 that the only physiological development its Vitamin Water was likely to provide was obesity from all the sugar. (The suit is still in progress.) In 2014, the makers of extreme energy drink Red Bull agreed to pay $13 million over charges of misleading advertising. Evidently Red Bull doesn't give you wings, even metaphorically. ●

MOLECULAR GASTRONOMY

"I may be the only chef in New York who has Dow Chemical as one of his purveyors."

— WILEY DUFRESNE

TIME OF ORIGIN: *1994*

ORIGIN IN: *El Bulli restaurant, Cala Montjoi, Spain*

HYPE FACTOR: *4 — When a trend only takes a decade before it's the secret behind the hottest restaurant in the world, well, then you know that people are taking notice.*

IMPACT FACTOR: *2 — Most restaurants still serve dishes that we can at least attempt to re-create at home.*

Is cooking an art or a science?

To the traditional gourmet, it is decidedly the former. But in our increasingly tech-driven times, one strain of kitchen iconoclasts has been focusing on the science.

The marriage of high cuisine and high technology is often called *molecular gastronomy.* The cooks who practice it, however, tend to be an unruly, individualistic lot and refer to themselves by many names. But whether self-identifying as kitchen scientists, the avant-garde, or simply modern cooks, these culinary explorers share some basic traits: a sense of play, an approach to food as an intellectual and technological challenge, and a compulsion to revisit classic dishes and, literally, to reengineer them.

FOAM BUBBLES TO THE FOREFRONT

Every food era has its emblem. In the '60s, it was the fondue pot. In the '70s, it was the Cuisinart. The '80s had the pasta machine, and in the '90s people fawned over the KitchenAid mixer. In the 2000s, the siphon bottle with nitrous oxide cartridge moved into ascendency.

For centuries, chefs had been whipping up fluffy concoctions like mousses and soufflés. Fat, from butter or cream, or protein, from egg whites, provided structure, while air whipped in with a metal whisk provided loft. But around the turn of the millennium, adventurous chefs borrowed an idea from industrial cookery and started substituting neutral-tasting stabilizers, like lecithin or an algae extract called *agar*.

The result was lighter-bodied foams whose flavor was cleaner, less diluted, and more suited to main dishes than their fat-based cousins, which tended to be relegated to the dessert course.

Culinary foam went from inspired novelty to embarrassing fad with all the speed of the nascent Information Age. Soon enough, anything that could be liquefied would be foamed — mashed fruit, vegetable purées, oyster liquor, sea urchin roe, herbal infusions, curry sauce. A new taxonomy had to be invented especially to capture all the nuances of texture and volume: *airs, bubbles, froths, espumas, puffs…*

On cooking competition TV shows, foam became the new secret weapon, displacing foie gras or shaved truffles as the magic addition that would take an ordinary dish "to the next level."

Collapsing from media overexposure, foam quickly became a laughingstock, a culinary novelty, a cheat. It was quietly retired before most diners had even tried it.

But a Rubicon had been crossed. Foam may not have endured, but the infiltration of science into the kitchen had just begun.

THE RESTAURANT THAT RULED THE AUGHTS

Culinary foam was pioneered by chef Ferran Adrià at Spain's El Bulli. Rising to chef de cuisine in 1987, Adrià had become increasingly experimental in his outlook throughout the '90s. His culinary creativity garnered his restaurant three Michelin stars. Between 2002 and 2009, El Bulli would go on to be chosen best restaurant in the world an unprecedented five times.

Ferran Adrià was the first internationally hailed practitioner of molecular gastronomy — a term introduced by food scientists in 1988.

Famously, Chef Adrià only kept his restaurant open for six months of the year. The rest of the time he spent developing recipes and inventing new techniques. The results were stunning (critics would say *pretentious* or *overdesigned*) presentations that appealed to the mind and the eye as much as the palate. For instance, Adrià took the humble Spanish tortilla, a potato cake bound with eggs and flavored with onion, and deconstructed it. He foamed the potatoes, puréed the onions, layered them with a thin custard called *sabayon*, and then served it in a tiny sherry glass — a nod to the cheap tapas bars the original recipe had come from.

Each year, one million hopeful diners would vie for just 8,000 spots. Some would fly in just for the experience of Adrià culinary surprises, such as olive oil transformed into caviar, Parmesan ice cream sandwiches, and martinis served in perfume vaporizers. As one food critic put it, dining at El Bulli "was the culinary equivalent of the Cirque du Soleil, complete with acrobats, magicians, and clowns."

Three-hour, 30-course sampling meals at $300 a head was all part of food culture during the economic boom years of the early 2000s, and El Bulli did not long outlive the bust: Adrià closed its doors in 2011. But scientific cookery was far from over.

MAD SCIENTISTS AND DISRUPTORS

The US has had its own disciples of molecular gastronomy. On these shores, however, the impresario-cum-magician persona that Chef Adrià cultivated is replaced by a more down-to-earth and techy vibe.

For instance, Wylie Dufresne, our most well-known scientific chef, might justly be described as a little dweeby. He's balding on top, but with long, lank hippie hair and sideburns, and has the soft-spoken air of a chemistry TA rather than a celebrity chef. (The name of his signature restaurant, wd~50, which unhappily lost its space in Manhattan's Lower East Side at the end of 2014, was an allusion to everyone's favorite mechanical lubricant, WD-40.)

On the other coast, the Seattle-based Nathan Myhrvold is a bona fide geek: The outspoken evangelist for modernist cuisine is a trained theoretical physicist and former chief technology officer at Microsoft. Though he is an amateur cook with no restaurant experience, Myhrvold's résumé and personal fortune have given him a considerable platform. In typical tech-mogul style, Myhrvold has led with an audacious outsider assault. His coauthored *Modernist Cuisine* is a six-volume work that presents a radically revised history of cooking from a scientific perspective. When the book was released in 2010, some of the nation's hottest chefs hailed it as revolutionary, while traditionalists started baying for blood.

Contemporary modern cuisine (if that's not redundant) has moved well beyond foams. Myhrvold's personal kitchen, like the former space at wd~50 and the facilities now at Chicago's Moto, recalls a miniature space station, stocked with vacuum sealers, sous vide poaching baths, quick-freeze anti-griddles, canisters of synthesized food additives, self-sustaining grow rooms, and even weapons-grade lasers and laboratory-ready centrifuges.

Flavor-wise, there is little uniting molecular gastronomy. Instead, the cuisine is characterized by restless innovation. At Moto, it takes the form of a constant search for new ingredients or old favorites treated in radically new ways — like their square watermelons, cultivated in plastic boxes, whose extra sweetness comes supposedly from water molecules that have been aligned from continual exposure to classical music. (There's sometimes a thin line between science and watermelon fertilizer.)

On the other hand, Chef Dufresne is more mad chemist than world explorer. His claim to fame is having found a way to fry mayonnaise — which, scientifically speaking, should explode in hot oil and then stick to your skin in gobs of superhot fat. Dufresne found a chemical work-around in the form of a powdered gum that stabilizes the mayo.

As a gentle poke in the eye to devotees of the farm-to-table movement that fetishizes whole foods and farmers' markets, Dufresne jokes that his kitchen contains everything you'd find listed on a bag of Doritos.

A FUTURE FOR MODERNIST EATING?

Although molecular gastronomy has shed its decadent trappings of bubble-economy excess, it is still an exclusive club. Despite its almost two-decade turn in the cultural spotlight, relatively few people have actually tried molecular cuisine. And since the scientific knowledge and apparatus it demands puts modernist cooking beyond the reach of the typical home

THE MOLECULAR KITCHEN

Sous vide: In this is a low-temperature cooking method, food is vacuum-sealed and cooked in an evenly heated water bath. Compared with fire cooking, sous vide is more gentle and even, and it prevents overcooking.

Anti-griddle: The smooth metal surface of this appliance can be set at low as –30° F. This allows chefs to freeze sauces, batters, and other foods quickly to bring a new palette of textures and temperatures to the dinner table.

Agar-agar: This is just one of many gels and thickeners that allow chefs to bind ingredients. This is the magic that brings us spaghetti made of arugula instead of flour and ice cream made from… just about anything.

Pop Rocks: This longtime candy favorite creates effervescence through a combination of sugar and carbon dioxide. Add moisture, and you get that familiar soda sizzle on your tongue. Molecular chemists keep Pop Rocks on hand to dust desserts with an explosive surprise.

cook, few may ever. Even with its volume on home cooking, it is unlikely that Myhrvold's 2,400-page opus, which retails for $650, will be sharing shelf space next to the *Joy of Cooking* in many homes.

But a generation of chefs has found inspiration in the experiments of molecular gastronomy. Whether it eventually filters down to neighborhood restaurants is yet to be seen. But don't write it off yet: After all, it took 20 years for the farm-forward philosophy of Alice Waters' legendary Chez Panisse to put mixed baby greens in every market in the nation.

Maybe the next kitchen emblem will be a chemistry book and a jar of xanthan gum. ●

9/11 AND THE END OF IRONY

"One good thing could come from this horror; it could spell the end of the age of irony."

— ESSAYIST ROGER ROSENBLATT, "THE AGE OF IRONY COMES TO AN END," 2001

TIME OF ORIGIN: *September 24, 2001*

ORIGIN IN: Time *magazine*

HYPE FACTOR: *9 — Blaming the 9/11 attacks on our obsession with superficial ironic posing gave a grieving nation a much-welcomed opportunity to indulge in our other great obsession, superficial moralistic posing.*

IMPACT FACTOR: *2 — Happily, the nation arose when it realized that giving up our precious irony would be allowing the terrorists to win.*

The collapse of the Twin Towers on September 11, 2001, was a unique moment in modern US history, when the entire nation was genuinely united in a shared experience of shock, grief, and outrage. For the space of a few weeks, all the normal divisions — political affiliation, race, class, degree of coolness — ceased to matter. We were all Americans joined in mourning.

Famously, Jon Stewart and David Letterman took their shows on hiatus. And when they returned, they opened with heartfelt reflections. The absence of distancing, self-protective laughter — of irony — was not a matter of good manners, a polite deferral to the gravity of the moment. In the immediate wake of the terrorist attack, the pain was too immediate: Irony was unthinkable.

9/11 AND THE END OF IRONY **199**

But people inevitably take things too far, and a sincere response to unspeakable tragedy became inflated into a decisive cultural shift: the End of Irony.

THE ENEMY WITHIN

Linguist and cultural critic Geoffrey Nunberg identified the first person to declare the death of irony in print as journalist Andrew Coyne, who made the call on September 12. But Coyne was Canadian, so it didn't count. Bigger news was made when New Yorker Graydon Carter also predicted irony's imminent demise. Given that it was coming from the publisher of *Vanity Fair* and *Spy* magazine, the '80s embodiment of disaffected irony, Carter's statement was sort of like the Pope declaring the end of Catholicism. But the person who gets the credit for really starting the "irony is dead" meme is essayist Roger Rosenblatt.

For a seminal text, Rosenblatt's essay hasn't aged well. Today it reads like such an angry, confused, and sad screed caught up in the overwhelming emotions of the moment that it feels almost churlish to hold the author to account for it. But the article is *really* dumb. As a stunned nation struggles to come to terms with the new and possibly endless era of violence and extremism it has been hurled into, the essayist decides that the *real* problem is those damned kids with their hipper-than-thou attitude. "The consequence of thinking that nothing is real — apart from prancing around in an air of vain stupidity — is that one will not know the difference between a joke and a menace. No more." It was our addiction to *Seinfeld* that had robbed the nation of its moral compass and made us unable to stop the 9/11 attacks.

Rosenblatt's provocation drew an immediate response from *Salon*, which argued that now, when feelings were so raw and the call to reactive violence so strong, now was exactly the time we needed some distance from our emotions: "We need a profoundly ironic outlook to avoid being swept up in the new jingoism."

The post-cataclysmic period of unity was officially over.

A PREMATURE BURIAL

The anti-ironists were sincere, but they were wrong. In fact, irony was already clawing its way out of the casket. A couple days after the attack, comedian Gilbert Gottfried broke the 9/11 taboo, telling an audience at a celebrity roast, "I have to leave early tonight. I'm flying to L.A. I couldn't get a direct flight. We have to make a stop at the Empire State Building." The joke fell flat. But by the end of the month, the late-night talk shows were back and daring us to laugh again. The first post-9/11 issue of *The Onion* (still on paper back then) offered irony of the highest order, with headlines that aired our emotional wounds while alleviating their sting with a spray of self-directed humor: "Not Knowing What Else to Do, Woman Bakes American-Flag Cake"; "American Life Turns into Bad Jerry Bruckheimer Movie."

What the moral scolds had missed is that irony is a time-tested method of dealing with the cruel incongruities of life. The times when our vision of what life should be is most at odds with a reality we cannot deny are the times when irony is both a comfort and a powerful means of resistance. It's no accident that irony flourished during the Cold War in the totalitarian nations behind the Iron Curtain.

Any lingering doubts about the longevity of irony were demolished on May 1, 2003, when a flight-suited president George W. Bush stepped out of a fighter plane and onto the deck of a battleship to announce, "Mission accomplished." It was less than two months into what would actually become the longest war in American history. ●

THE SEGWAY

"It won't beam you to Mars or turn gold into lead. So sue me."

— DEAN KAMEN, ON HIS INVENTION THE SEGWAY HT

TIME OF ORIGIN: *Climaxed on December 3, 2001*

ORIGIN IN: *Officially unveiled in Bryant Park, New York*

HYPE FACTOR: *7 — The hype was intense but relatively brief.*

IMPACT FACTOR: *1 — Aside from becoming a hackneyed punch line, the Segway has not had much of an effect — not yet, at any rate.*

In the realm of innovation, it is not enough to have an excellent product. You have to have a good story too. Successful technologists, like Kodak's George Eastman and Apple's Steve Jobs, are great seducers, fast-talkers who can convince consumers that they possess previously unknown needs that can be met only with a new camera or cell phone.

The disastrous debut of the Segway scooter was one of the major marketing missteps of the twenty-first century. It also shined an instructive light onto the peculiar combination of hubris and naiveté that can characterize the thinking of our new techno-entrepreneur overlords. For people that smart, they sure can act dumb.

BEHIND THE HYPE

A college dropout with more that 440 patents to his credit, inventor and futurist Dean Kamen deserves his reputation for being an eccentric genius. He started inventing at the age of 16, when he made a device that allowed lights to respond to sound. While still in college, he developed a portable drug-infusion pump. Then he followed it up with the first portable insulin pump, a portable dialysis machine, and a variety of stents that increase blood flow in clogged arteries and help prevent them from bursting. At the age of 30, Kamen sold his medical device factory for $30 million. With the funds, he created DEKA, his own research and development lab now staffed with some 400 engineers.

Kamen also has a well-earned reputation for living like a James Bond super-villain. Aside from running his own top-secret laboratory, he owns his own island off the coast of Connecticut, a three-acre site called North Dumpling. Claiming that he has seceded from the US, Kamen styles himself as the island's feudal ruler, Lord Dumpling, and has created his own flag and currency. Everyone assumes he's joking. But nobody's sure.

Lord Dumpling — Dumpie to his friends — owns two helicopters, two jets, and an amphibious landing craft. And, not unlike the late tech über-guru Steve Jobs, who was never seen without his signature charcoal mock turtleneck, Kamen has his own uniform — blue jeans, hiking boots, and work shirt. Sure, it lacks the flair of the bespoke Mao suits favored by James Bond's archnemesis, Ernst Stavro Blofeld — but at least Kamen can get the White House to return his phone calls, without having to threaten to blow up the world.

In 2001, hardly anyone outside the tech community had heard of Dean Kamen. But in January of that year, rumors began to circulate that the eminent innovator was on the brink of unveiling something really big. How big?

How about bigger-than-the-Internet big?

CODE NAME: IT, AKA GINGER

It was venture capitalist John Doerr who claimed that Kamen's new invention was going to be bigger than the Internet. That was according to a secret book proposal that was leaked in January 2001. The book, written by journalist Steve Kemper, who had had a behind-the-scenes view of Kamen's latest device, was sold to Harvard Business School Press for a purported $250,000 (which is an *awful* lot more than this book sold for. Just saying…).

Doer had made a fortune from Amazon.com and Netscape, the first major Internet browser, so his opinion mattered to people who follow

Wall Street. An opinion that mattered even more to the general public was Steve Jobs', and he was on record speculating that Kamen's new product — sometimes referred to as *IT*, other times as *Ginger* — just might be bigger than the PC.

With those tantalizing clues, speculation abounded. Was IT a cold-fusion device? A hovercraft? A superefficient, low-emissions engine? A perpetual-motion machine?

Kamen, who was absorbed in the final stages of his project, refused to comment — which only fueled speculation.

From the beginning, however, there was evidence suggesting IT would be some sort of scooter. Kamen had already perfected the iBot, a super-wheelchair that could rear up without tipping over and even climb stairs — abilities that had led DEKA engineers to give the device the (incredibly lame) code name *Fred Upstairs*, after dancer Fred Astaire, star of countless classic MGM musicals. *Ginger*, the code name of Kamen's new invention, recalled Astaire's dance partner, Ginger Rogers, which, to many prognosticators, suggested the device would be some variation of the iBot. Indeed, a number of academics and tech insiders reported seeing prototypes of some personal transporter derived from the iBot.

But a scooter, though? IT couldn't be just that. Right? It had to be hydrogen-powered. Or maybe it floated using a form of magnetic antigravity.

MAXIMUM SEGWAY

On December 3, 2001, Dean Kamen appeared on *Good Morning America* in a segment shot in New York's Bryant Park to unveil… a scooter. A scooter that looked a lot like a very large push lawnmower.

To give the invention its due, the Segway HT (for *H*uman *T*ransport) is a remarkable piece of engineering. Its tilt sensors monitor the rider's center of gravity more than 100 times per second. Riders lean forward to accelerate and backward to stop, but the response is so quick and so subtle that many say it's like thought control. The Segway cruises at between five and 17 miles per hour, but the standard setting is eight miles an hour — a little more than twice a fast walking pace. The battery-powered, low-emissions engine allows the vehicle to travel 17 miles on a single charge at a cost of about 10 cents. If it hadn't been so hyped, people might have been impressed.

Claiming his invention would be to the car what the car was to the horse and buggy, Kamen went on to appear on *The Tonight Show* and got not only host Jay Leno but also actor Russell Crowe and the intensely humorless musician and activist Sting to take a ride. And the hype continued. Segway rose to 14 on Yahoo's Buzz Index. Niles, the dweeby younger brother on the popular comedy show *Frasier*, rode the new scooter in one of its episodes, and the December 17 issue of the *New Yorker* featured a cartoon Osama bin Laden tooling around the hills of Tora Bora on a Segway. Both *The Daily Show* and *The Onion* got their digs in too. But *South Park* beat them all by deriding "IT" hype in the episode "The Entity," which aired a month *before* Segway debuted.

THE PERFECT SOLUTION NOBODY WANTED

Kamen was getting an incredible amount of free publicity, but in his previous months of silence he had lost control of the narrative. And when he tried to regain it, his hyperbolic statements and technocratic attitude often alienated audiences. The Segway was designed to be an ecologically sound means of filling the transportation gap between driving and walking. This was a laudable goal, but within a week of debuting his product, Kamen had managed to antagonize drivers, walkers, and bikers — pretty much everyone who had a stake in transportation.

A more serious oversight was that Kamen had seemingly done no market research. Weighing 60 pounds and selling for $5,000, the Segway was awkward, ugly, and unaffordable. When Kemper's book on the Segway backstory was published, it was revealed that Steve Jobs' first impression of the device was that "it sucks." He was referring to the design, and he was correct. The Segway possesses a seemingly magical power to make any rider look supremely dorky.

Kamen had raised an estimated $90 million to fund his venture, and his Segway company was valued at $650 million before he'd even sold a single scooter. In eight years, however, he sold only an estimated 50,000 Segways, slightly more than the 40,000 his factory was capable of producing in a month.

In 2009, Kamen quietly sold his Segway company to a British company backed by a businessman named Jimi Heselden. The next year, Heselden died in a Segway accident.

If the Segway were an ancient artifact, we'd be sure there was a pharaoh's curse on it. ●

APPLE IPHONE

"Today, we're introducing three revolutionary products... The first one is a widescreen iPod with touch controls. The second is a revolutionary mobile phone. And the third is a breakthrough Internet communications device... These are not three separate devices. This is one device. And we are calling it iPhone."

— APPLE INC. COFOUNDER AND CEO, STEVE JOBS, INTRODUCING HIS COMPANY'S DEBUT SMARTPHONE

TIME OF ORIGIN: *January 9, 2007*

ORIGIN IN: *Macworld Expo, San Francisco*

HYPE FACTOR: *10 — With each successful product launch, Apple CEO Steve Jobs was increasingly regarded as delivering not sales pitches but holy writ. This veneration climaxed during the early iPhone era.*

IMPACT FACTOR: *9 — While history has yet to judge whether the information revolution will be as transformative as many claim, the move from home-based PCs to mobile computing is definitely a revolution within a revolution.*

In the mid-'90s, when the Internet was starting to explode and PC ownership was rapidly becoming the norm in American households, Apple computer was in deep trouble. By then the cult favorite, which had won accolades for introducing the first graphics-based user interface for home computing with its 1984 Macintosh machine, had cemented a reputation for producing well-designed, easy-to-use products... that nobody used. High price tags and a limited roster of software — both the consequences of cofounder Steve Jobs's obsessive and controlling quest for perfection —

had consigned Apple products to single-digit market share in the late '80s and almost drove the company out of business.

Instead, the company drove out Jobs. But when Apple's fortunes failed to improve, the board of directors eventually invited Jobs back. After an 11-year exile, the new CEO resuscitated Apple, releasing the iMac in 1998 and the iPod three years later. But the most transformational device of Jobs's second tenure at Apple was the iPhone.

Originally envisioned as an iPod that could make calls, the iPhone is really a telephone in name only. By getting rid of the bulky and restrictive keyboard, the iPhone's multitouch interface, run by a powerful operating system, took full advantage of smartphone technology, transforming the device into a genuine handheld computer.

Nearly 25 years after introducing in the next big thing in personal computing, Apple disrupted its own model by pushing the move to mobile computing.

SMOKE, MIRRORS, AND GORILLA GLASS

Tech demos are models of disingenuousness. A presenter — almost inevitably a conspicuously casually dressed, young to middle-aged guy — wearing a lapel mike walks an audience of eager techies through the features of his cool new toy. Ostensibly, it's all off the cuff and relaxed. In reality, the spiel is meticulously choreographed to high-kick the features while sidestepping the bugs.

Steve Jobs was a master of the form. In his signature mock turtleneck and dad jeans, his John Lennon glasses, and cropped top like that of a Buddhist monk, the futurist-entrepreneur conveyed just the right mix of intensity, nerdy tech-cred, and wholehearted, geeky enthusiasm for gadgetry.

Jobs's showmanship skills were never in greater demand than on the morning opening of the 2007 Macworld Expo. That year Apple had one product to premier: the iPhone, the company's first smartphone. And the product didn't work.

The apps were buggy and the phone was prone to crash. You could send an email and then surf the Web — but not the other way around. Calls were frequently dropped, and, although Apple had convinced AT&T to install a portable cell tower right in San Francisco's Moscone Center, engineers took the extra precaution of rigging the phone to display five full bars of signal strength, regardless of the actual connection.

In front of an audience of reporters and industry insiders, Jobs put the iPhone through its paces according to a well-rehearsed "golden path" — the single arrangement that could demo all the features without crashing the device.

The presentation went off without a glitch. Even if it hadn't, though, the iPhone was destined to impress. With its face a featureless monolith of black, specially made, ultra-hard "gorilla glass," the iPhone was the first device to employ a multitouch interface that dispensed with keyboards and bothersome styluses. It was elegant, efficient, and cool as hell. As happens from time to time, the world was once again reminded of what it is to love a machine.

Assembled in the audience, the heart of the iPhone engineering team had been surreptitiously downing shots of whiskey to steady their nerves. By the end of the presentation they were blotto, intoxicated not just from booze but from relief, jubilance at the overwhelming audience response, and from sheer exhaustion.

"YOU CALL THIS THE PHONE OF THE FUTURE?"

Apple came late to the cell phone market and with a large dose of anxiety. By convention, cell phone design was a three-way collaboration between a hardware maker, a software maker, and a phone carrier — with the last party wielding the lion's share of influence. The standard practice was to regard the phones themselves as flashy toys whose main purpose was to lock consumers into long-term contracts with phone companies. Jobs, a notorious control freak, loathed the idea of deferring to a phone company executive and of compromising his product for the sake of someone else's business plan.

On the other hand, Apple's killer product was the iPod, a single-feature device that did nothing but play music. As smartphone technology was advancing, Jobs recognized that it would just be a matter of time before competitors would be able to add their own MP3 apps to their devices and throttle Apple's cash cow that was earning nearly half of the company's revenue.

Apple's first foray into cell phones was a 2005 collaboration with the manufacturer Motorola and the wireless carrier Cingular. The result, the Rokr, was one of Apple's rare utter disasters. Although it was the first phone to come equipped with iTunes, the device was clumsy, slow, and had an arbitrary limit of just 100 songs. On top of that, it was super ugly and had a really, really dumb name.

Hyping a merciless review, *Wired* magazine put the Rokr on its cover under the headline "You Call This the Phone of the Future?"

Mortified by the Rokr, Jobs resolved to go it alone: For its smartphone, Apple would make both the software and the hardware, and its presentation would live up to the company's reputation for impeccable design. In the months leading up to the iPhone demo, the Apple campus, which has long enjoyed a reputation for having a certain *Lord of the Flies* atmosphere even in the best of times, was especially taught. Jobs's A team was subjected to sleepless nights, frayed nerves, and temper tantrums all the way down the chain of command. One project manager reportedly slammed the door to her office so hard that the latch stuck, and she was rescued only after colleagues battered the door handle with an aluminum baseball bat. It was probably the only enjoyment they'd felt in weeks.

AN INESCAPABLE WEB

In *Zardoz*, John Boorman's marvelously bonkers science-fiction film from 1974 (which stars a hairy-chested Sean Connery swaddled in nothing more than an orange loincloth, knee boots, and crossed bandoliers), the pampered and privileged elite of a post-apocalyptic utopia dress like hippies and talk like British aristocrats. They are also linked to each other by means of enormous crystal rings each wears, which give free access to everybody's thoughts and memories as well as the storehouse of all human knowledge and artistic achievement. In this world of complete connectivity, the desire for privacy is viewed as intolerable selfishness and an insult to the community.

We might not sport unisex shag haircuts today, but increasingly we are linked to everyone we know — not through crystals but through the cloud. Almost 60 percent of adults in this country own a smartphone; for the under-30 set, the number jumps to 83 percent. According to a 2013 study commissioned by Facebook, however, found that only 16 percent of smartphone communications are phone calls. The rest is Internet-based activity — texting, email, and social media posts.

To think of a smartphone as a telephone then is to miss its actual importance: For increasing numbers of us, our smart device is our supplemental brain, our Zardoz ring. It's our telecommunications device, our reference collection, library, music and video catalogue, personal photo album—and it fits in our pocket and goes wherever we do.

We can only speculate whether Steve Jobs found inspiration in *Zardoz*, but when he was pioneering the idea of the digital hub that would conveniently synch a user's data — from photos, videos, and music to email, documents, and contact lists — to and from an array of devices, the "hub" for him was a PC. But the development of smarter smartphones and the massive storage capacity of the cloud has made a stationary, home-based PC nerve center unnecessary.

Always-connected handhelds, wearables, and an inundation of cheap or free apps sending endless streams of information into the cloud is certainly the short-term vision for technology. Whether these conveniences will generate enduring value is another question. The success of an app such as the car service Uber demonstrates the potential of this new field to generate money and to disrupt business as usual. And yet Uber's service — ordering cabs by phone — is hardly revolutionary. And Uber is not the only app that essentially duplicates an existing service by moving it online.

More troubling are the privacy concerns created by mobile computing. As more of our lives are lived online, companies with access to our browsing information know more and more about us. Who owns that information, what they can do with it, and what rights we have over it will continue to be pressing questions—particularly as data seemingly becomes the one thing that can be assuredly monetized in the digital era.

Whatever the future of mobile computing, for simply providing navigation apps that eliminate the need to ask for directions ever again, the iPhone deserves at least nine impact points. ●

THE MICROBIOME

"So who am I? Ed Yong, a human defined by my body and my genome? Or am I a vehicle for bacteria? Am I one individual or an entire universe? I think it is the latter."

— SCIENCE WRITER ED YONG

TIME OF ORIGIN: *2008*

ORIGIN IN: *National Institutes of Health*

HYPE FACTOR: *4 — For scientists this might register as an 8, but for the rest of us, microbiome has yet to become a household word.*

IMPACT FACTOR: *4 — We still don't know how much of an impact our understanding of the microbiome might have on medicine — but so far it looks like a promising area of study!*

Ever since 1862, when Louis Pasteur's experiments with heating milk proved the link between bacteria and disease, humankind's take on microorganisms has been bracingly simple: *bacteria bad.* More recently, however, biologists have discovered that each of us carries around our own unique set of microorganic life and that, far from being our mortal foes, microorganisms fulfill essential functions in our bodies.

A radically new approach to disease is now emerging, whose central insight turns traditional medicine on its head: What if the secret to good health is not ridding ourselves of microorganisms but actually making ourselves better hosts for them?

SO CRAPPY TO MEET YOU

On the morning of July 10, 2010, thousands of unsuspecting *New York Times* readers seated at their breakfast tables were treated to a side order of poop.

Science writer Carl Zimmer was reporting the story of a woman suffering from debilitating diarrhea. But wait, there's more: Although antibiotics had proven useless in her case, the afflicted women had found an unpalatable cure: an infusion *of her husband's feces*!

This somewhat paradoxical and utterly disgusting intervention is called *fecal transplantation*, or, more euphemistically, *bacteriotherapy*, and it is founded on the conjecture that a healthy digestive system depends on an equilibrium of native microorganisms. When the body's microflora are devastated, say by a powerful course of antibiotics following an operation, occasionally certain strains will recover first and proliferate at the expense of others. Unchecked, these normally harmless denizens of the gut can run rampant and cause serious disturbances, like chronic dysentery.

However, transplanting a healthy microbial mix en masse to the gut can restore its natural balance. The culprits behind the dysentery are not eradicated, but, under some mysterious influence of their microbial peers, these disgruntled microbes settle down to become peaceable members of the intestinal community once more.

The problem is, no one knows exactly what belongs in the gut: There are simply too many types of microorganism — far more than have even been observed, let alone named. But there is an easy solution. Human poop is made up mostly of bacteria. Obtain a stool sample from anyone, and all it takes is some careful filtering to unveil a Noah's ark of the donor's intestinal microbes waiting to go forth and repopulate a desolated gut.

For at least a decade, this fringy fecal therapy had been a recurring feature in small-market newspapers and local television stations in need of a weird news piece. But Zimmer's article was its first appearance in the nation's newspaper of record.

BETTER KNOW YOUR MICROBIOME!

- Credit for discovering the microbiome goes to Antoni van Leeuwenhoek, the seventeenth-century Dutch lens grinder who also brought us the microscope. Scraping the film from his teeth and viewing it beneath his new invention, Leeuwenhoek observed that "there were many very little living animalcules, very prettily a-moving. The biggest sort… had a very strong and swift motion, and shot through the water (or spittle) like a pike does through the water."
- For every cell of human we posses, each of us carries *ten* microorganisms. If the body were a democracy, the Human Party would be *almost* as outnumbered as Republicans are in New York City.
- Only 40 percent of your poop is digested food; the rest is microorganisms.
- The microbiome is often referred to as "microflora." Technically, however, this is a kingdomist misnomer that covers only plant life, like yeasts, while ignoring all the billions of other members of our extrahuman community that are bacteria, viruses, or archaea.

What was the difference this time? A $150 million initiative backed by the National Institutes of Health called the Human Microbiome Project (HMP). Initial reports from the HMP suggested that, indeed, the microorganisms that make a home of us are not just random aggregations of hitchhikers. They work together to form an ecosystem. And while elements can go rogue and threaten our health, far more often these germs are performing essential jobs for us — like breaking down foods our stomach cannot digest and refining our immune systems.

The fringy ideas behind bacteriotherapy were starting to look less fringy.

A MICROSCOPIC CENSUS

Dazed by the ick factor of Zimmer's article, many readers might have overlooked the real news: something called the *microbiome*.

The term, which was coined in 2001 by microbiologist Joshua Lederberg, refers to the ecological community of microorganisms — good, bad, and indifferent — that dwell on and inside us.

It had long been recognized that each of us is host to some 100 trillion microorganisms — that's ten times the number of cells that make up our bodies. But we knew hardly anything about them because microbes are notoriously hard to study. Many are so well adapted to their particular niche in the human body that they cannot survive laboratory conditions.

New developments in microbiology, however, allowed a new approach to studying microbes. Instead of having to capture or culture them, microorganisms could also be inventoried by genetic analysis. Samples could be taken from, say, someone's mouth. Strands of DNA could then be extracted and a certain gene compared. Any variation there would indicate a different type of life form.

It was now possible to take a rough census of the microorganisms anywhere on anyone. And these findings could be compared with other samples to produce a genetic map of the human biome, just as the human genome had been mapped during the 1990s.

In fact, it was scientists who had worked on the Human Genome Project who lobbied the National Institutes of Health to create the Human Microbiome Project. They argued that their map of the human genome would be incomplete until we understood the synergetic relationship between our bodies and the trillions of microorganisms that are continually interacting with us.

AN OUTSOURCED ORGAN

Under the auspices of the HMP, 200 researchers at 80 locations are analyzing data gathered from some 250 volunteers.

Just over 11,000 samples have been taken, but each is so teeming with genetic material that working with the complete data is beyond the scope of any existing computer.

A full report is slated for release in 2015. Despite the complexity of the challenge, however, findings have been trickling out. One surprise is that there is no such thing as a typical human microbiome. Each of us is born sterile, but as soon as we're out of the womb, we start collecting our individual microbiome, one that reflects our unique history — every place we've visited, every morsel of food we've eaten, every piece of crud we put into our mouths as babies.

It gets even creepier than that: Our microbiome can indicate what way we were delivered (that is, whether we were delivered via C-section or not) and whether we were breast-fed.

Although microorganisms have colonized many parts of our bodies, they abound in our intestines, where they help us digest our food and even play a role in how much and what kind of nutrients we absorb. Initial research suggests that microbes may affect our risk of bowel disease and allergies, our inclination to weight gain and infection.

The services our microbiome provides are so specific and so essential that scientists have likened it to a hidden organ. Perhaps it is more accurate to look at it as an outsourced organ. Just as businesses regularly operate across national borders, our lives, in a sense, transcend our human cells.

It is no exaggeration to say that we each are our own planet Earth, providing a multitude of microclimates within the warm, acid oceans of our guts, the salty oases of sweat glands, our jungle armpits and cavernous stretches of mucus membrane.

Even if no cures are directly indicated by the HMP's final report, it will likely move us conceptually to a radically new way of looking at ourselves. •

BIBLIOGRAPHY

ALCOHOL

Dietler, Michael. "Driven by Drink: The Role of Drinking in the Political Economy and the Case of Early Iron Age France." *Journal of Anthropological Archaeology* 9, no. 1 (1990): 352–406.

Kahn, Jeffrey P. "How Beer Gave us Civilization." *New York Times*, March 15, 2013.

McGovern, Patrick E. *Uncorking the Past: The Quest for Wine, Beer, and Other Alcoholic Beverages.* Berkeley: University of California Press, 2009. [kindle]

THE CHARIOT

Anthony, David W. *The Horse, the Wheel, and Language: How Bronze-Age Riders from the Eurasian Steppes Shaped the Modern World.* Princeton, N.J.: Princeton University Press, 2007.

Anthony, David W. "Two Indo-European Phylogenies, Three Proto-Indo-European Migrations, and Four Kinds of Steppe Pastoralism." *Journal of Language Relationship*, no. 9 (2013).

Anthony, David W., and Dorcas R. Brown. "The Secondary Products Revolution, Horse-Riding, and Mounted Warfare." *Journal of World Prehistory* 24, no. 2 (2011). doi: 10-1007/s10963-011-9051.9

Barbieri-Low, Anthony J. "Wheeled Vehicles in the Chinese Bronze Age (c. 2000–741 B.C.)." Edited by Victor H. Mair. *Sino-Platonic Papers* (University of Pennsylvania), no. 99 (February 2000).

Cameron, Alan. *Circus Factions: Blues and Greens at Rome and Byzantium.* Oxford: Oxford University Press, 1976.

Drews, Robert. *The End of the Bronze Age: Changes in Warfare and the Catastrophe ca. 1200 B.C.* Princeton, N.J.: Princeton University Press, 1993.

Procopius. *The Secret History.* Translated by G. A. Williamson. New York: Penguin Books, 1981.

RELIGION AS PERSONAL FAITH

Brown, Peter. *The Making of Late Antiquity.* Cambridge, Mass.: Harvard University Press, 1978.

Burkert, Walter. *Greek Religion.* Translated by John Raffan. Cambridge, Mass: Basil Blackwell Publisher and Harvard University Press, 1985.

Burkert, Walter. *Mystery Cults.* Cambridge, Mass.: Harvard University Press, 1987.

SINGLE-POINT PERSPECTIVE

Alberti, Leon Battista. *On Painting.* Translated by John R. Spencer. Rev. ed. New Haven: Yale University Press, 1962.

Berger, Harry, Jr. *Second World and Green World: Studies in Renaissance Fiction-Making.* First paperback ed. Berkeley: University of California Press, 1990.

Panofsky, Erwin. *Meaning in the Visual Arts.* Phoenix edition. Chicago: University of Chicago Press, 1982.

THE MOVABLE TYPE PRINTING PRESS

British Library. "Treasures in Full: Gutenberg Bible." Accessed Sept. 4, 2014. http://www.bl.uk/treasures/gutenberg/homepage.html.

Pettegree, Andrew. *The Book in the Renaissance.* Kindle edition. New Haven: Yale University Press, 2010.

University of Göttingen. "Gutenberg Digital Project." Accessed Aug. 30, 2014. http://www.gutenbergdigital.de/gudi/start.htm.

THE DIVINE RIGHT OF KINGS

James I, King of England. *The Political Works of James I.* Edited by Charles Howard McIlwain. Cambridge: Harvard University Press, 1918.

MAGNETIC PHILOSOPHY

Baldwin, Martha. "Magnetism and the Anti-Copernican Polemic." *Journal for the History of Astronomy* 16, no. 3 (1985).

McMullin, Ernan. "Moving the Earth." *HOPOS: The Journal of the International Society for the History of Philosophy of Science* 1, no. 1 (Spring 2011): 3–22.

Pumfrey, Stephen, and Nigel Goose. "William Gilbert: Forgotten Genius." *Physics World*, November 1, 2003.

Zilsel, Edgar. "The Origins of William Gilbert's Scientific Method." In *The Social Origins of Modern Science*, edited by Robert Cohen and Marx Wartofsky. Dordrecht, Netherlands: Kluwer Academic Publishers, 2003.

THE GREAT MASCULINE RENUNCIATION

Kremer, William. "Why Did Men Stop Wearing High Heels?" *BBC News Magazine*, January 24, 2013. http://www.bbc.com/news/magazine-21151350.

Kuchta, David. "The Making of the Self-Made Man: Class, Clothing, and English Masculinity, 1688–1832." In *The Sex of Things: Gender and Consumption in Historical Perspective*, edited by Victoria de Grazia with Ellen Furlough, 54–78. Berkeley: University of California Press, 1996.

SCIENTIFIC RACISM

Fabian, Ann. *The Skull Collectors: Race, Science, and America's Unburied Dead.* The University of Chicago Press, 2010.

Gossett, Thomas F. *Race: The History of an Idea in America.* New Edition. New York: Oxford University Press, 1997.

THE KODAK CAMERA

Cohan, Peter. "How Success Killed Eastman Kodak." *Forbes*, October 1, 2011. http://www.forbes.com/sites/petercohan/2011/10/01/how-success-killed-eastman-kodak.

Lindsay, David. "The Wizard of Photography." *The American Experience.* http://www.pbs.org/wgbh/amex/eastman/index.html.

FREUDIANISM

Gay, Peter. "Sigmund Freud: A Brief Life." In *New Introductory Lectures on Pschyo-Analysis,* by Sigmund Freud. Translated by James Strachey. New York: W.W. Norton and Co., 1989.

Menand, Louis. "Head Case: Can Psychiatry Be a Science?" *New Yorker*, March 1, 2010.

Rabin, Roni Caryn. "A Glut of Antidepressants." *New York Times*, August 12, 2013.

Samuel, Lawrence R. *Shrink: Psychoanalysis in America.* Lincoln: University of Nebraska Press, 2012.

PLASTICS

Freinkel, Susan. "A Brief History of Plastic's Conquest of the World." *ScientificAmerican.com*, May 29, 2011. http://www.scientificamerican.com/article/a-brief-history-of-plastic-world-conquest/.

Moore, Charles. "Trashed: Across the Pacific, Plastics, Plastics, Everywhere." *Natural History,* v. 112, n. 9. Nov. 2003.

New York Times. "Host of New Uses in Plastics Shown." April 23, 1946.

National Geographic. *Great Pacific Garbage Patch.* 7 Feb. 2015. <http://education.nationalgeographic.com/education/encyclopedia/great-pacific-garbage-patch/?ar_a=1>.

Powers, Vivian. *The Bakelizer.* Washington, D.C.: American Chemical Society, 1993.

Thompson, Richard C., Shanna H. Swan, Charles J. Moore, and Frederick S. vom Saal. "Our Plastic Age." *Philosophical Transactions of the Royal Society B,* June 15, 2009. *http://rstb.royalsocietypublishing.org/content/364/1526/1973.full.*

THE DANCE CRAZE

Cardell, Roy L. "The City of Dreadful Dance." *New York World.* March 30, 1913.

Chapman, Beverly A. "New Dance in New York, 1911–1915" (master's thesis, American University, 1977).

Erenberg, Lewis A. *Steppin' Out: New York Nightlife and the Transformation of American Culture, 1890–1930*. Chicago: University of Chicago Press, 1981.

Noble, Richard B. Report 15 July 1916. Committee of Fourteen Papers. Special Collections, New York Public Library.

THE TEENAGER

Palladino, Grace. *Teenagers*. New York: Basic Books, 1996.

ROCK 'N' ROLL

Altschuler, Glenn C. *All Shook Up: How Rock 'n' Roll Changed America*. New York: Oxford University Press, 2003.

Fong-Torres, Ben. "Biography of Alan Freed." Alan Freed official website. Accessed Aug. 13, 2014. http://www.alanfreed.com/biography.

Freed, Alan. "Alan Freed Says: 'I Told You So…'" *Down Beat*, September 19, 1956. http://www.alanfreed.com/archives/archives-rocknroll-1951-1959/newspaper-magazine-clippings.

Irwin, Theodore. "Rock 'n Roll'n Alan Freed," *Pageant*, July 1957. http://www.alanfreed.com/archives/archives-rocknroll-1951-1959/newspaper-magazine-clippings.

3-D MOVIES

Baughman, James L. "Television Comes to America, 1947–'57." *Illinois History* 46, no. 3 (March 1993). http://www.lib.niu.edu/1993/ihy930341.html.

Gil, Ricard, and Ryan Lampe. "The Adoption of New Technologies: Understanding Hollywood's (Slow) Conversion to Color, 1940–70." Stanford Institute for Economic Policy Research. *http://siepr.stanford.edu/system/files/shared/color%20movies.pdf*.

Lane, Anthony. "Third Way: The Rise of 3-D." *New Yorker*, March 8, 2010.

Stock, Kyle. "Fewer People Are Seeing Movies, but Box Office Revenue Is Up." *Businessweek*, March 26, 2014. http://www.businessweek.com/articles/2014-03-26/fewer-people-are-seeing-movies-but-box-office-revenue-is-up.

TV DINNERS

Dixon Lebeau, Mary. "At 50, TV Dinner Is Still Cookin'." *Christian Science Monitor*. November 10, 2004. http://www.csmonitor.com/2004/1110/p11s01-lifo.html.

Ferdman, Roberto A. "America Is Falling Out of Love with TV Dinners." *Atlantic*, March 13, 2014.

Gasparro, Annie. "Frozen Foods Grow Cold as Tastes Shift to Fresher Fare." *Wall Street Journal*, June 26, 2014.

Gust, Lauren. "Defrosting Dinner: The Evolution of Frozen Meals in America." *Intersect: The Stanford Journal of Science, Technology & Society* 4, no. 1 (2011).

Library of Congress. "Who 'Invented' the TV Dinner? Everyday Mysteries: Fun Science Facts from the Library of Congress, August 23, 2010. http://www.loc.gov/rr/scitech/mysteries/tvdinner.html.

Maksel, Rebecca. "He Saved Navy Fliers from Spam." *AirSpaceMag.com*, May 17, 2012. http://www.airspacemag.com/daily-planet/he-saved-navy-fliers-from-spam-98327183/?no-ist.

Schwartz, Brie. "The History of the TV Dinner." *Gourmet Live*, October 19, 2011. http://www.gourmet.com/food/gourmetlive/2011/101911/the-history-of-the-tv-dinner.

Shapiro, Laura. *Something from the Oven: Reinventing Dinner in 1950s America*. New York: Penguin Books, 2004.

Story, Louise. "Gerry Thomas, Who Thought Up the TV Dinner, Is Dead at 83." *New York Times*, July 21, 2005.

THE PILL

Comstock, Anthony. *Traps for the Young*. New York: Funk & Wagnalls Co., 1883.

Eig, Jonathan. Interview by Terry Gross. *Fresh Air*, National Public Radio, October 7, 2014.

Gibbs, Nancy. "The Pill at 50: Sex, Freedom, and Paradox." *Time*, April 22, 2010.

Laurence, William L. "Life Is Generated in Scientist's Tube." *New York Times*, March 27, 1936.

Rubin, Rita. "The Pill: 50 Years of Birth Control Changed Women's Lives," *USA Today*, May 8, 2010.

Tone, Andrea. *Devices and Desires: A History of Contraceptives in America*. New York: Hill and Wang, 2001.

SYNTHETIC FOOD

Beck, Julie. "Soylent, Meal Replacements, and the Hurdle of Boredom." *Atlantic,* April 30, 2014.

Belasco, Warren. "Future Notes: The Meal-in-a-Pill." *Food in the USA: A Reader,* ed. Counihan, Carole M. Routledge, 2002

Dam, Henry J.W. "Foods in the Year 2000." *McClure's Magazine,* Sept. 1894, p. 303–312.

Dodd, Anna Bowman. *The Republic of the Future.* New York: Cassell, 1887; downloaded: https://archive.org/details/republicofthefut00doddrich

NASA. "Space Food Hall of Fame." Last modified January 27, 2014. http://education.ssc.nasa.gov/fft_halloffame.asp.

Widdicombe, Lizzie. "The End of Food: Has a Tech Entrepreneur Come Up With a Product to Replace Our Meals?" *The New Yorker,* May 12, 2014.

EASY LISTENING

Lanza, Joseph. *Elevator Music*. New York: St. Martin's Press, 1994.

THE MIDLIFE CRISIS

Sheehy, Gail. *Passages: Predictable Crises of Adult Life.* New York: Bantam Books, 1977.

Wethington, Elaine. "Expecting Stress: Americans and the 'Midlife Crisis'." *Motivation and Emotion.* Vol. 24, No. 2, 2000.

TV CONSOLE GAMES

Baer, Ralph. "Genesis: How the Home Video Games Industry Began." Ralph Baer official website. Accessed Dec. 14, 2014. http://www.ralphbaer.com/how_video_games.htm.

Douglas, Martin. "Ralph H. Baer, Inventor of the First System for Home Video Games, Is Dead at 92." *New York Times*, December 7, 2014. http://nyti.ms/1CWNdEl.

Edwards, Benj. "The Right to Baer Games—An Interview with Ralph Baer, the Father of Video Games." *Gamesutra*, March 23, 2007. http://www.gamasutra.com/view/feature/130108/the_right_to_baer_games__an_.php.

Isaacson, Walter. "The Birth of Pong." *Slate*, October 17, 2014. http://www.slate.com/articles/technology/technology/2014/10/the_invention_of_pong_how_nolan_bushnell_launched_the_video_game_industry.html.

Kamenetz, Anya. "Why Video Games Succeeded Where the Movie and Music Industries Fail." *Fast Company*, November 7, 2013. http://www.fastcompany.com/3021008/why-video-games-succeed-where-the-movie-and-music-industries-fail.

Mullis, Steve. "Inventor Ralph Baer, the 'Father of Video Games,' Dies at 92." *All Tech Considered*, NPR, December 8, 2014. http://www.npr.org/blogs/alltechconsidered/2014/12/08/369405270/inventor-ralph-baer-the-father-of-video-games-dies-at-92.

Statt, Nick. "Video Game Industry Grew 4 Times Faster Than US Economy in 2012, Study Says." CNET, November 11, 2014. http://www.cnet.com/news/video-game-industry-grew-4-times-faster-than-us-economy-in-2012-study-says.

Watters, Ethan. "The Player: Atari. Pong. Chuck E. Cheese. Nolan Bushnell Launched the Age of the Videogame. Now He Wants to Save the World from Grand Theft Auto." *Wired*, October 2005. http://archive.wired.com/wired/archive/13.10/bushnell_pr.html.

METRICATION

Ford, Gerald. "Statement on Signing the Metric Conversion Act of 1975." December 23, 1975. The American Presidency Project. AccessedMarch 5, 2014. www.presidency.ucsb.edu/ws/?pid=5454.

Gallup, George. "Public Remains Cool to Metric Conversion." *Lexington Dispatch*, November 24, 1977, 5. http://news.google.com/newspapers?nid=1734&dat=19771124&id=THoqAAAAIBAJ&sjid=mFEEAAAAIBAJ&pg=6562,2308288.

Judson, Lewis V. *Weights and Measures Standards of the United States: A Brief History.* NBS Special
   Publication 447; U.S. Dept. of Commerce, National Bureau of Standards, Washington, D.C.,
   1963; updated 1976.

THE BOOM BOX

Oatman-Stanford, Hunter. "How Boomboxes Got So Badass." *Collectors Weekly*, December 16, 2013.
   http://www.collectorsweekly.com/articles/how-boomboxes-got-so-badass.
Owerko, Lyle. *The Boombox Project.* Kindle edition. New York: Abrams Image, 2010.

THE WALKMAN

Alexander, Ron. "Stereo-to-Go—and Only You Can Hear It." *New York Times*, July 1, 1980.
Fantel, Hans. "An Era Ends as Cassettes Surpass Disks in Popularity." *New York Times*, November 21,
   1982.
Haire, Meaghan. "A Brief History of the Walkman." *Time*, July 1, 2009. http://content.time.com/
   time/nation/article/0,8599,1907884,00.html.
Joseph, Raymond A. "Hey, Man! New Cassette Player Outclasses Street People's 'Box.'" *Wall Street
   Journal*, June 23, 1980.
Knox, Andrea. "Digital Tape Has Become Audio's New War Zone." *Philadelphia Inquirer*, November
   30, 1986.
Nathan, John. *Sony: The Private Life.* New York: Houghton Mifflin, 1999.
Sony. "Just Try It." Sony Corporate History. Accessed Jan. 4, 2015. http://www.sony.net/SonyInfo/
   CorporateInfo/History/SonyHistory/2-06.html.
Swensson, Andrea. "40 Years of Album Sales Data in Two Handy Charts." *The Current* (blog),
   KCMP-FM, Minnesota Public Radio. http://blog.thecurrent.org/2014/02/40-years-of-album-
   sales-data-in-one-handy-chart.
Zito, Tom. "Stepping to the Stereo Strut: On the Run with the Sony Walkman." *Washington Post*,
   May 12, 1981.

PROZAC

Elliott, Stuart. "A New Campaign by Leo Burnett Will Try to Promote Prozac Directly to
   Consumers." *New York Times,* July 1, 1997.
Fitzpatrick, Laura. "A Brief History of Antidepressants." *Time*, January 7, 2010.
Freudenheim, Milt. "The Drug Makers Are Listening to Prozac." *New York Times*, January 9, 1994.
Greenberg, Gary. "The Psychiatric Drug Crisis." *New Yorker*, September 3, 2013.
Kramer, Peter D. *Listening to Prozac.* New York: Viking, 1993.
Kramer, Peter D. Letter to the editors. *New York Review of Books*, July 14, 1994.
Menand, Louis. "Head Case: Can Psychiatry Be a Science?" *New Yorker*, March 1, 2010.
Metzner, Richard J. "Prozac Is Medicine, Not a Miracle." *Los Angeles Times*, March 14, 1994.
Newsweek. "The Culture of Prozac." February 6, 1994.
Nuland, Sherwin B. "The Pill of Pills," *New York Review of Books*, June 9, 1994.

THE END OF HISTORY

Atlas, James. "What Is Fukuyama Saying? And to Whom Is He Saying It?" *New York Times,* Oct. 22,
   1989.
Fukuyama, Francis. "The End of History?" *The National Interest,* Summer 1989.

NC-17

Grimes, William. "Reviewing the NC-17 Film Rating: Clear Guide or an X by a New Name?" *New
   York Times*, November 30, 1992.
Maslin, Janet. "Is NC-17 an X in a Clean Raincoat," *New York Times*, October 21, 1990.
Rohter, Larry. "Resistance to NC-17 Rating Develops." *New York Times*, October 13, 1990.